D0461312

big kevin **little kevin**

big kevin **little kevin**

Over 120 recipes from around Britain
and America by TV's Odd Couple

Kevin Woodford
and **Kevin** Belton

EBURY PRESS
LONDON

DEDICATION

Kevin Woodford: To my wife Jean for her creativity and inspiration whilst working alongside me developing and testing recipe ideas. Not only did she ensure that they were technically sound, but more importantly that they taste great! Also not forgetting my beautiful daughter Janine, son Steven and future daughter in law Gemma.
Kevin Belton: For my sons Kevin II and Jonathan, who allowed me to leave home long enough to complete the television series.

First published in 1999

1 2 3 4 5 6 7 8 9 10

By arrangement with the BBC. Based on the BBC Television Programme

First published in the United Kingdom in 1999 by Ebury Press
Random House, 20 Vauxhall Bridge Road, London SW1V 2SA

Random House Australia (Pty) Limited
20 Alfred Street, Milsons Point, Sydney,
New South Wales 2061, Australia

Random House New Zealand Limited
18 Poland Road, Glenfield, Auckland 10, New Zealand

Random House South Africa (Pty) Limited
Endulini, 5a Jubilee Road, Parktown 2193, South Africa

Random House UK Limited Reg. No. 954009

Papers used by Ebury Press are natural, recyclable products made from wood grown in sustainable forests.

A CIP catalogue record for this book is available from the British Library.
ISBN 0 09 186513 1

Designed by Alison Shackleton
Food photography by Philip Webb
Other photography by Andrew Fettis, Susan Grimshaw and Faith Penhale
Food styling by Dagmar Vasely and Oona van den Berg

Printed and bound in the United Kingdom by Butler and Tanner Ltd, Frome and London

CONTENTS

INTRODUCTION

Coming into Tobermory, Mull, after an afternoon of diving for scallops.

It all began on my first visit to New Orleans, to make a holiday programme with Carol Smillie. We were filming the tourist spots of the city and I wanted to include something on food. New Orleans is a food-crazy place, with restaurants on every street corner and people munching Po-Boys at every turn (French bread sandwiches, all a poor boy could afford in the old days).

We ended up at the New Orleans School of Cookery, where we were thoroughly entertained by big Kevin Belton and, of course, well fed. I had been wanting to make a comparison programme between the UK and North America for years and finally I found the man to hold up the American end – and at 6′ 9″ and 22 stone he could certainly hold up quite a lot.

On the other side of the pond, in the UK, was another chef I knew well – Kevin Woodford. With the difference in size being so great and in name so little, the title of the programme was obvious.

What we set out to do was to look at great regional food across the British Isles and

America – food that was identifiable from its source; places where people were still trying to get the best from the land, not just the most. We discovered that so many comparisons could be made that we were spoilt for choice, so we picked areas that had obvious links. Some of these were food links, such as the story of the chilli in Mexico and in Bradford. Some were geographically similar, like the mountain landscape of Wales and Montana, and others were linked by their respective histories, such as Scotland and Nova Scotia (New Scotland).

Sunset at Cape Breton.

The Old World meets the New in the kitchen.

On our journey, we found that food producers 5,000 miles apart faced the same problems, and we discovered people who were devoting their lives to the best food imaginable – people we could not fail to admire. We found the typical, we found the extraordinary, we were surprised and amused but, best of all, we found truly great food.

Andrew Fettis
Series producer

LONDON AND

Taking a ride on an old-fashioned brewer's dray from Fuller's Brewery in Chiswick, London.

In the past ten years, London has dragged itself out of the gutter from a culinary point of view. In the past some would say that London has followed New York for its gastronomic style, but now London is brave enough to stand on its own two feet.

It is in these two cities that food can be the most accurately compared between the nations: places where both tastes and style are of the moment, magnified as though under some great spotlight from one of the stages in Broadway or the West End. It is here that one can say with some confidence that Americans like this and the British like that, although ultimately taste is always a personal preference.

These are cities with great chefs, each pulling their country's gastronomy along in unique directions, each educating their clientele with new ways, ideas and styles. All this filters down to street level, so that food traders are caught short when everyone demands sweet basil one day and salad burnet the next.

NEW YORK

ABOVE: A host of Italian sausages, hung up to dry, in New York's Little Italy.

Mixed with this food fashion are the traditions, the way things used to be and, some argue, still ought to be. The traditionalists provide basic good food, something that is always in fashion. Once you grasp this mix of the old and the new, you start to realise what food and cooking are all about in both London and New York.

BELOW: Mark Felderman of Russ and Daughters in New York's Lower East Side.

crabby **new york** salad

Fresh crab always makes this a great treat, but if relatives come round unexpectedly just use canned crab meat.

SERVES 8

900 g (2 lb) lump crab meat
6 tbsp mayonnaise
1 tbsp Dijon mustard
1 tsp curry powder
1 tbsp cayenne pepper
juice of 1 lemon
1 large sweet onion, chopped
1 red pepper, deseeded and chopped
1 yellow pepper, deseeded and chopped
salt and freshly ground black pepper
endive leaves, to serve

Mix the crab meat, mayonnaise, mustard, curry powder and cayenne pepper in a large bowl. Mix well, seasoning to taste with salt and pepper. Pour in the lemon juice and stir in the chopped onion and red and yellow peppers. Serve on endive leaves.

KB

smoked **eel salad** on toasted granary bread

Sometimes, all you feel like is a light, tasty, nutritious snack which doesn't take too much energy to make. This is it!

SERVES 4–6

225 g (8 oz) crème fraîche
2 tbsp Dijon mustard
175 g (6 oz) smoked eel fillets
juice of 1 lemon
50 g (2 oz) chicory leaves, finely shredded
50 g (2 oz) spring onions, white only, finely shredded
1 tbsp chopped dill
6 slices granary bread
3 tbsp extra-virgin olive oil
2 cloves garlic, crushed
salt and freshly ground black pepper
paprika, to garnish

Mix together the crème fraîche and the Dijon mustard. Flake the eel into bite-sized pieces and add to the mixture. Add the lemon juice, chicory, spring onions and dill. Season with salt and freshly ground black pepper.

Toast the granary bread, drizzle a little olive oil over and spread the crushed garlic on top.

Pile the smoked eel salad on the bread, dust with a little paprika and serve.

KW

green mayo with **smoked fish** salad

The smoked fish at Russ & Daughters in New York was so great that I had to combine it with my favourite food, mayonnaise. This recipe extracts the great flavours of the herbs and looks good too. When I mentioned to Mark from Russ & Daughters that I was going to put mayonnaise on his fish, he shuddered and told me no New York Jewish family would do that, so once you've made 'the green' you could add it to cream cheese and serve with a hot bagel.

SERVES 8

FOR THE MAYONNAISE
2 egg yolks
250 ml (8 fl oz) olive oil
1 tsp lemon juice
salt and freshly ground black pepper

FOR 'THE GREEN'
175 g (6 oz) baby spinach
115 g (4 oz) rocket
50 g (2 oz) fennel tops
50 g (2 oz) fresh parsley
50 g (2 oz) fresh chervil
50 g (2 oz) fresh tarragon
25 g (1 oz) fresh coriander
25 g (1 oz) spring onions

FOR THE SMOKED FISH SALAD
900 g (2 lb) smoked fish, such as salmon, sturgeon, halibut, or chub
1 large sweet onion, chopped
1 yellow pepper, deseeded and chopped
1 red pepper, deseeded and chopped
1 fennel bulb, chopped
rocket leaves
endive leaves

Make the mayonnaise; beat the seasoned egg yolks whilst slowly drizzling in the oil until thick and glossy, add the lemon juice and continue whisking.

Remove all stalks before weighing, then blend all the leaves and herbs in a food processor. Transfer the well-processed leaves to a square of cheesecloth, bundle them up and squeeze to extract as much liquid as possible. Warm the liquid over a low heat and just before it starts to simmer take off the heat and strain through cheese cloth stretched over a bowl. When well strained take the purée left behind on the cheesecloth and mix with the mayonnaise.

Arrange the fish and chopped vegetables on the salad leaves and dress with the green mayonnaise.

KB

grilled asparagus with chervil vinaigrette

I have a huge appetite for good vegetables prepared properly. So if I'm coming round to dinner ... don't overcook the asparagus!

SERVES 8

1 tbsp chopped fresh chervil
1 shallot, diced
2 tbsp fresh lemon juice
½ tsp salt
¼ tsp cracked black pepper
5 tbsp olive oil
900 g (2 lb) asparagus stalks, peeled
225 g (8 oz) mozzarella cheese, cut into 1cm/½ inch slices
fresh chives, to garnish

In a bowl, mix together the chervil, shallot, lemon juice, salt and pepper. Slowly whisk in 3 tbsp of the olive oil.

In a pan of boiling water, blanch the asparagus for 1 minute.

Place the asparagus in a shallow dish and sprinkle with the remaining 2 tbsp olive oil. Make sure all asparagus are coated with oil.

Heat a cast-iron griddle pan over a high heat and grill the asparagus a few at a time until tender and lightly browned.

To serve, place the asparagus on individual plates and top with a slice of mozzarella. Spoon a little chervil vinaigrette over the top and garnish with the chives.

KB

sun-dried **tomato** and **basil** soda scones

These scones are wonderful, try and use buttermilk as this really gives a rich flavour.

SERVES 4–6

225 g (8 oz) flour
1 tsp baking powder
1 tsp salt
1 tsp finely chopped sun-dried tomato
1 tsp finely chopped basil leaf
1 egg
1 tsp melted butter
159 ml (¼ pint) buttermilk (or full cream milk, if you really have to)

Sift the flour, baking powder and salt into a medium-sized mixing bowl and then add the sun-dried tomato and basil and gently mix.

Beat the egg and mix in the melted butter and buttermilk.

Make a well in the centre of the flour mixture and pour in buttermilk mixture. Stir gently to form a soft dough and roll out lightly on a floured surface until the dough is about 2 cm/¾ inch thick.

Using a 5 cm/2 inch scone cutter, cut as many scones as you can. Place the scones on a greased and floured baking sheet and cook in a preheated oven at 220°C/425°F/Gas 7 for 10–15 minutes.

KW

butternut squash with cardamom and cinnamon

If you like a sweet taste, then sprinkle a little brown sugar in the bowl when tossing the squash with butter.

SERVES 8

1.5 kg (3 lb) butternut squash, peeled, seeded and cut into cubes
6 cardamom pods, crushed
6 whole cloves
3 cinnamon sticks, broken in half
3 bay leaves
20 g (¾ oz) butter, unsalted
salt

In a bowl, toss the butternut squash with cardamom, cloves, cinnamon and bay leaves. Bring water to a boil in a large steamer and add the seasoned squash. Cover and steam for about 15 minutes or until tender. Remove the cardamom, cloves, cinnamon sticks and bay leaves. Place the squash in a bowl and toss with the butter. Season to taste and serve.

KB

king prawns with pak choi

We as a nation have developed a taste for king prawns and this spicy little dish takes our delight to the point of ecstasy!

SERVES 4

3 tbsp olive oil
1 stem lemon grass, outer leaves removed, stem halved and bruised
3 cloves garlic, finely sliced
zest and juice of 2 limes
5 cm (2 inch) fresh ginger root, peeled and thinly sliced
2 tbsp chopped fresh coriander
1 red pepper, deseeded and sliced
1 green pepper, deseeded and sliced
225 g (4 oz) red onion, thinly sliced
1 hot red chilli, deseeded and thinly sliced
450 g (1 lb) king prawns, peeled
225 g (8 oz) pak choi, cut into small pieces
75 g (3 oz) fine green beans
75 g (3 oz) mange-tout
3 tbsp Nam Pla (fish sauce)
salt and freshly ground black pepper

Heat the oil in a wok; add the lemon grass, garlic, zest of limes, ginger, coriander, red and green peppers, red onion and chilli.

Cook for 3–4 minutes, add the prawns and remaining vegetables; cook for a further 4–5 minutes.

Remove the lemon grass stem, season with the fish sauce, lime juice, salt and freshly ground black pepper. Serve immediately.

KW

gratinated **courgette dumplings** with a basil and tomato sauce

A lovely dish and a firm favourite amongst my vegetarian friends. Whilst courgettes can be quite bland, when used as a base in this recipe they lend themselves nicely as a host for the other flavours – giving body and texture to the finished dish.

SERVES 4–6

4 courgettes, roughly chopped
175 g (6 oz) Parmesan cheese, grated
small bunch fresh coriander
5 cloves garlic, crushed
pinch of nutmeg
400 g (14 oz) ricotta cheese
275 g (10 oz) plain flour, sifted
4 tbsp olive oil
75 g (3 oz) shallots, finely diced
450 g (1 lb) plum over-ripe tomatoes, peeled, deseeded and chopped
120 ml (4 fl oz) dry white wine
1 tbsp sun-dried tomato purée
1 tsp Tabasco sauce
½ tbsp Worcestershire sauce
pinch of sugar
50 g (2 oz) white breadcrumbs
2 tbsp chopped parsley
salt and freshly ground black pepper

Place the courgettes in a microwave oven and cook on high for about 3 minutes. Transfer to a food processor, add half the Parmesan, the coriander and half the garlic. Blend until the mixture is coarse in texture. Place in a fine sieve over a bowl and allow the excess liquid to drain through, lightly press to ensure that most of the liquid is removed.

Place the courgette mixture in a clean bowl, add the nutmeg, ricotta and mix thoroughly. Fold in the flour and season with salt and lots of freshly ground black pepper. Cover and chill.

To make the sauce, heat the olive oil in a saucepan, add the shallots and remaining garlic; cook for 2 to 3 minutes until soft but not coloured. Add the chopped tomatoes and wine and bring to the boil; add the tomato purée and reduce the heat. Simmer the mixture gently for 5 to 8 minutes. Season with Tabasco and Worcestershire sauce, and salt and pepper. Add a pinch of sugar, stir, cover and keep warm.

Bring a wide shallow pan of water to the boil, season with salt and allow to simmer. Using 2 teaspoons, mould the dumpling mixture into oval egg shapes (if the mixture is too wet add a little extra flour and mould the shapes using floured hands). Gently place the dumplings in the hot water and cook until they rise to the surface. Remove from the pan and drain on kitchen paper.

Place the dumplings in a lightly buttered ovenproof dish and pour the tomato sauce over. Mix the breadcrumbs, parsley and remaining Parmesan. Sprinkle over the top of the dumplings and place under a hot grill until the topping becomes brown. Serve immediately.

KW

fettuccine **alla carbonara**

Thanks to people like Mr Mario Borghatti, in New York's Little Italy you can find truly superb fresh pasta, and that's the trick to this simple dish, beautiful fresh pasta. The sauce won't overpower the pasta, so its taste can shine through.

SERVES 4

8 rashers bacon
175 g (6 oz) sliced prosciutto
175 g (6 oz) unsalted butter
25 g (1 oz) chopped onion
450 g (1 lb) fettuccine
5 tbsp white wine
120 ml (4 fl oz) whipping cream
120 ml (4 fl oz) milk
1 tbsp chopped parsley
40 g (1½ oz) Parmesan cheese, grated
1 egg yolk
freshly ground black pepper

In a large frying pan, cook the bacon and drain it thoroughly. Cut the prosciutto and bacon into 1 cm/½ inch squares. Melt the butter in a saucepan; add the onion and sauté over a low heat until the onion is translucent.

Meanwhile, cook the pasta in a large pan of boiling salted water until al dente.

Add the bacon and prosciutto to the onion and stir over low heat for 3–4 minutes. Pour in the wine and bring the mixture to a boil for 5 minutes, stirring. Add the cream and milk and bring to a slow boil again for 5 minutes. Lower the heat, add the parsley and half of the Parmesan.

Pour the cream sauce over the drained pasta. Add the egg yolk and toss thoroughly. Add the remaining Parmesan and freshly ground black pepper to individual portions.

KB

blackened salmon with oven roasted vegetables

A spicy dish that always impresses dinner guests and although big Kev objects to me claiming this style of cooking fish, it does reflect the cosmopolitan influences in London. Anyway just because he's bigger than me, it doesn't mean he should win every argument!

SERVES 4

1 tbsp crushed black peppercorns
1 tbsp dried oregano
1 tsp dried rosemary
1 tbsp dried thyme
2 tbsp paprika
1 tbsp cumin
1 tbsp sea salt
4 portions filleted salmon
4 plum tomatoes, halved
2 courgettes, cubed
1 aubergine, cubed
115 g (4 oz) Kenyan beans, blanched
1 red pepper, deseeded and cut into chunks
129 ml (4 fl oz) olive oil
1 tbsp chopped fresh coriander
2 tbsp chopped fresh basil
50 g (2 oz) black olives, pitted and quartered
4 tbsp balsamic vinegar
freshly ground black pepper

Using either a pestle and mortar or a food processor, mix together the peppercorns, dried herbs and sea salt. Transfer the mixture to a flat dish. Press the salmon fillets, skin side down into the mixture and place to one side.

Put the tomatoes on a bed of sea salt and place in a preheated oven at 190°C/375°F/Gas 5 for 45 minutes. After 10 minutes add the courgettes, aubergine, blanched beans and red pepper. Drizzle with about half of the olive oil and return to the oven.

Heat a little oil in a frying pan, add the salmon, spice side down and cook over a high heat until it blackens. Turn it over and cook for a further 2–3 minutes. Remove from the pan, cover and keep warm.

Remove the vegetables from the oven, sprinkle the coriander, basil and black olives over the vegetables, season with black pepper and add the balsamic vinegar.

Serve the salmon, blackened side up, on top of the vegetables and spoon the cooking liquid from the vegetables around the serving dish.

KW

breast of **duck** with **beetroot** in sour cream

This is a rich dish for those important occasions when you want something particularly special. The beetroot and duck work really well to produce a surprising medley of flavours.

SERVES 4

3 tbsp olive oil
450 g (1 lb) red onions, sliced
2 cloves garlic, crushed
1 inch fresh ginger root, finely chopped
4 duck breasts
150 ml (¼ pint) red wine
150 ml (¼ pint) port
zest and juice of 2 oranges
zest and juice of 1 lemon
2 tbsp soft brown sugar
250 ml (8 fl oz) sour cream (or crème fraîche if you prefer)
225 g (8 oz) fresh beetroot, peeled, blanched and thinly sliced
salt and freshly ground black pepper

Heat the oil in a sauté pan, add the onions and cook slowly for 10 minutes, until they soften and colour. Then add the garlic and ginger and cook gently for a further 10 minutes.

Season the duck breasts and place on a preheated griddle pan, skin side down. Cook over a high heat for 2–3 minutes to colour the skin. Turn the duck over and place in a preheated oven at 200°C/400°F/Gas 6 for 12–15 minutes. Allow to rest for 5 minutes.

Add the wine, port, orange and lemon juice and grated zests to the onions and bring to the boil. Add the sugar, cook for a further 10 minutes until most of the liquid has been reduced. Add the sour cream, beetroot and mix well.

To serve, place the beetroot mixture on the plates, carve the duck breasts into slices and arrange on top.

KW

sausage and **mash** with a spiced onion gravy

One of my all time childhood favourites; the addition of a stronger sausage and a spiced gravy makes it a treat for adults too.

SERVES 4

- 350 g (12 oz) potatoes, cubed
- 175 g (6 oz) swede, cubed
- 115 g (4 oz) carrots, diced
- 115 g (4 oz) unsalted butter, cut into 4 cubes
- 2 leeks, sliced
- 3 tbsp olive oil
- 450 g (1 lb) sausages, your favourites (mine are venison)
- 115 g (8 oz) onions, finely sliced
- 2 cloves garlic, crushed
- ¼ tsp cardamom
- ¼ tsp cayenne pepper
- ½ tsp ground coriander
- freshly grated nutmeg
- ¼ tsp Tabasco sauce
- ½ tsp Dijon mustard
- 1 glass red wine
- 300 ml (½ pint) chicken stock
- 50 g (2 oz) butter, chilled
- salt and freshly ground black pepper

Cook the potatoes, swede and carrots in a pan of boiling salted water for 15–20 minutes until cooked.

In a small pan, melt ¾ of the cubed unsalted butter, add the chopped leeks, season with salt and pepper and cook gently for 15 minutes.

Meanwhile, heat the olive oil in a frying pan and cook the sausages. Remove from the pan, cover and keep warm.

Put the sliced onions in the same frying pan, add the last cube of unsalted butter, crushed garlic, cardamom, cayenne, coriander and cook for 5–8 minutes.

Drain the potatoes, swede and carrot mixture. Replace in the pan and heat over a low heat to dry out. Mash and season with salt, pepper and grated nutmeg; add the cooked leeks, cover and keep hot.

To the onions, add the Tabasco sauce, mustard, red wine and chicken stock. Bring to the boil and reduce by one third. Whisk in the chilled butter and check the seasoning.

To serve, pile the mash high on the plates, cut each sausage in half at a 45° angle and place on top of the mash. Spoon a little of the onion sauce over the sausage and around the plate.

KW

creamy port **veal chops**

Clean as you cook with this recipe so that after you eat you can retire to your favourite chair for the afterglow. If you cannot get fresh mushrooms you can use dried; just soak them in chicken stock for an hour before using.

SERVES 4

50 g (2 oz) unsalted butter
4 French cut veal chops
25 g (1 oz) flat mushrooms, sliced
25 g (1 oz) shiitake mushrooms, sliced
25 g (1 oz) oyster mushrooms, sliced
120 ml (4 fl oz) port
120 ml (4 fl oz) whipping cream
120 ml (4 fl oz) chicken stock
2 tbsp chopped shallots
1 tbsp chopped parsley
cracked black pepper

Heat the butter in a large sauté pan and sauté the veal chops for 8–10 minutes on each side. Place the chops in the oven at 110°C/225°F/Gas ¼ to keep warm. To the dripping in the sauté pan, add the mushrooms and sauté for 3–5 minutes. Sir in the port, cream, chicken stock and shallots. Bring to a boil and boil until thickened, stirring constantly. Spoon the sauce over the veal chops, sprinkle with cracked black pepper and chopped parsley.

KB

lamb baked in a salt crust pastry

This is a very impressive dish for your dinner guests and it can be prepared in advance. The timing of the cooking allows for the lamb to be pink. If you prefer your meat well done, then bake for a further 5 minutes.

SERVES 4

4 tbsp olive oil
1.5 kg (3½ lb) best end of lamb, filleted, with bones chopped for stock
75 g (3 oz) onion, chopped
75 g (3 oz) carrot, chopped
75 g (3 oz) celery, chopped
50 g (2 oz) leek, chopped
4 ripe tomatoes
25 g (1 oz) tomato purée
1 litre (1¾ pints) chicken stock
bouquet garni
115 g (4 oz) fresh white breadcrumbs
50 g (2 oz) parsley, chopped
25 g (1 oz) thyme leaves, finely chopped
1 clove garlic, crushed
2 tbsp Dijon mustard
1 egg, beaten
freshly ground black pepper

FOR THE PASTRY

200 g (7 oz) plain white flour
175 g (6 oz) coarse sea salt
1 tbsp each fresh thyme and rosemary leaves, chopped
1 large egg, beaten
1 egg yolk

Heat 2 tbsp of the olive oil in a deep casserole, add the lamb bones and brown for a few minutes. Place in a preheated oven at 200°C/400°F/Gas 6 for 30 minutes. Remove from the oven, add the onion, carrot, celery and leek, and cook on the stove over a medium heat for 5 minutes.

Add the tomatoes, tomato purée, chicken stock and bouquet garni. Bring to the boil, skim off any impurities that rise to the surface and then simmer the stock for 1 hour.

Make the pastry by mixing together the flour and the sea salt. Add the herbs, egg and egg yolk. Mix the ingredients to form a smooth dough. If the dough feels too dry, add a little cold water, alternatively if it is too wet add a little flour. The dough must not be too wet. Cover the pastry with clear film and place in the refrigerator for at least 1 hour to allow it to rest.

Meanwhile, place the breadcrumbs, parsley, thyme leaves and garlic in a large bowl and blend slowly, adding enough oil to bind the ingredients together. Roll the pastry into a rectangle. Heat a little oil in a frying pan, season the fillets with freshly ground black pepper and seal quickly on all sides. Remove and dry on kitchen paper. Spread a little Dijon mustard over the fillets and roll them in the breadcrumb mixture.

Place the fillets in the centre of the pastry and roll up, covering the meat. Tuck under the edges and brush with beaten egg. Cook in a preheated oven at 220°C/425°F/Gas 7 for 10 minutes. Strain the stock and boil rapidly to reduce by two thirds. Check and if necessary adjust the seasoning.

To serve, cut open the pastry, lift out the fillets and carve them on a plate. Surround with neat egg shaped portions of mashed potato with goat's cheese and bacon (see page 106), and wilted spinach, and spoon a little stock around the dish.

KW

orange and mascarpone creams with a caramel sauce

Oranges give this dish real depth of flavour, however the recipe will work with any citrus fruit, thus enabling you to create different variations of this pudding using other fruits and liqueurs.

SERVES 6

juice of 4 oranges
2 leaves gelatine
6 x 6 cm (2½ inch) discs of sponge cake
115 g (4 oz) caster sugar
finely grated zest of 1 orange
3 egg yolks
250 g (9 oz) mascarpone cheese
250 ml (8 fl oz) whipping cream, lightly whipped
3 tbsp Cointreau
7 tbsp cold water
275 g (10 oz) granulated sugar
6 tbsp hot water
icing sugar and cocoa powder, to decorate

In a small pan, heat three quarters of the orange juice until it has reduced by half; set aside.

Soak the gelatine leaves in a little cold water. Place the sponge discs in the bases of six 6 cm/2½ inch ring moulds.

To make the mascarpone cream custard, put the caster sugar in a bowl and add the grated orange zest. Pour on the egg yolks and whisk vigorously until the mixture doubles in size and becomes pale in colour. Lightly whip in the mascarpone cheese and then gently fold in the whipped cream.

Pour the remaining orange juice into a pan. Squeeze and discard the excess liquid from the gelatine and place the soaked gelatine leaves in the orange juice. Gently warm, stirring until dissolved, and then strain the liquid into the mascarpone cream custard and gently mix through. Finally, add the Cointreau a little at a time.

Spoon a little of the reduced orange juice over the sponge bases and fill the moulds with the mascarpone cream custard and chill in a refrigerator for 3 hours until lightly set.

Make the caramel sauce; add the measured cold water to the granulated sugar and gently boil in a deep pan until the mixture becomes golden brown. Carefully add the measured hot water and allow to cool.

To serve, carefully remove the moulds, dust the top of the puddings with icing sugar and cocoa powder. Drizzle a little caramel sauce around the plates.

KW

banana brûlée

As a child, bananas and custard was without doubt my all time favourite pudding. This recipe takes the concept a delicious stage further and will be popular as a tea time treat for youngsters, as well as a dessert for those who have a slightly more sophisticated palate.

SERVES 4

250 ml (8 fl oz) whipping cream
150 ml (¼ pint) milk
½ vanilla pod, split
7 egg yolks
225 g (8 oz) unrefined caster sugar
2 bananas, sliced lengthways
unrefined caster sugar, for glazing

To make the custard, place the cream, milk and vanilla pod in a small saucepan and bring to the boil. In a bowl, whisk together the egg yolks and sugar. Once blended, pour on the hot liquid a little at a time to ensure that the mixture does not curdle, stirring continuously.

Using a teaspoon, scoop out the small seeds from the bananas (this will help eliminate any discoloration). Blend the bananas in a food processor until smooth and add to the custard.

Sieve the banana custard into 6cm/2½ inch ramekin dishes and cook in a preheated oven at 110°C/225°F/Gas ¼ for 45–60 minutes, until the top has just set but there is still a little movement when shaken. Remove from the oven, allow to cool and refrigerate for at least 4 hours.

To serve, cover the top with a fine coating of unrefined caster sugar and glaze, either by using a blow torch, ensuring that you move it around to spread the heat uniformly; or, place the ramekins under a hot grill and move the dishes around until an even colour is achieved.

KW

carrot cake

Kevin Woodford and I shared a piece of carrot cake from every menu we could find it on during our travels. I guess we were looking for the ultimate piece. I am not sure it exists, but this is a sure-fire contender.

SERVES 12

350 ml (12 fl oz) vegetable oil
400 g (14 oz) soft dark brown sugar
4 eggs
225 g (8 oz) flour, sifted
2 tsp cinnamon
2 tsp baking soda
2 tsp baking powder
115 g (4 oz) walnut pieces
450 g (1 lb) carrots, shredded

FOR THE ICING
225 g (8 oz) cream cheese
115 g (¼ lb) butter
375 g (13 oz) icing sugar
2 tsp vanilla essence

Mix the oil and sugar, beating well. Add 1 egg at a time and mix thoroughly. Add the sifted flour, cinnamon, baking soda and baking powder and mix well. Add the walnuts and shredded carrots.

Spoon the mixture into a greased 20 cm/8 inch loose bottomed cake tin and bake in a preheated oven at 180°C/350°F/Gas 4 for 50–60 minutes.

Mix all of the ingredients for the icing until well combined. Once the cake has cooled, spread the icing thickly over the top of the cake.

KB

amaretto **cheesecake**

As well as pasta, Italian immigrants brought amaretto liqueur with them to New York. Be careful, eat one piece of this cheesecake at a time!

SERVES 12

FOR THE CRUST
75 g (3 oz) Graham cracker crumbs*
2 tbsp sugar
1 tsp cinnamon
50 g (2 oz) melted butter

FOR THE CHEESECAKE
675 g (1½ lb) cream cheese, softened
200 g (7 oz) sugar
4 eggs
5 tbsp Amaretto

FOR THE TOPPING
225 g (8 oz) sour cream
1½ tbsp sugar
1 tbsp Amaretto
25 g (1 oz) toasted flaked almonds
5 g (2 oz) grated chocolate

Combine the Graham cracker crumbs, sugar, cinnamon and butter, mixing well. Press the mixture into the base and sides of a 23 cm/9 inch springform tin.

With a mixer, beat the cream cheese until light and fluffy. Gradually add the sugar and mix well. Add the eggs one at a time, beating well after each addition. Stir in the Amaretto, and pour the mixture into the prepared tin. Bake at 190°C/375°F/Gas 5 for 45 minutes or until set.

Combine the sour cream, sugar and 1 tbsp Amaretto, mix together and spread over the top of the cheesecake. Bake at 240°C/475°F/Gas 9 for 5 minutes. Allow to cool and refrigerate for 24 hours. Decorate with the almonds and chocolate.

*If you cannot get Graham crackers, use ginger nuts or Digestive biscuits.

KB

strawberry **coconut squares**

These are great to keep in the freezer – my sons have this as an after-game snack.

MAKES 30

FOR THE CRUST
16 Graham crackers*
175 g (6 oz) flour
200 g (7 oz) sugar
115 g (4 oz) unsalted butter, cut up
2 large eggs

FOR THE FILLING
275 g (10 oz) strawberry jam
115 g (4 oz) unsalted butter, softened
200 g (7 oz) sugar
2 large eggs
350 g (12 oz) shredded or grated coconut

Make the crust; crush the Graham crackers into fine crumbs. In a bowl mix the crumbs, flour and sugar. Add the butter and blend until mixture resembles coarse breadcrumbs. Beat the eggs in a separate bowl and add to the crumb mixture, blending with a fork. Press the mixture evenly into a 30 x 45 cm/12 x 18 inch Swiss roll tin.

Spread the jam over the crust. With an electric mixer, beat the butter and add the sugar, beating until light and fluffy. Add 1 egg at a time to mix well. Add the coconut and beat until well combined. Drop the coconut mixture a spoonful at a time over the jam and spread carefully to make an even coating.

Bake in a preheated oven at 180°C/350°F/Gas 4 for 20 minutes or until golden brown. Cool in the tin on a rack. Allow to chill for 1 hour before cutting into squares.

*If you cannot get Graham crackers, use ginger nuts or Digestive biscuits.

KB

CORNWALL

On the Helford river in Cornwall, about to go and get oysters.

What could these two areas possibly have in common? Although what the people put on their plates could not be more different, their attitude to food and the reasons they eat what they eat are remarkably similar. In fact, of all the locations these two have the most in common, if you ignore the fact that you are not going to find alligators in Cornwall or pilchards in Louisiana.

Both are physically cut off from their mother countries and, perhaps as a consequence, are amongst the poorest areas in their respective countries. Cornwall is a peninsula jutting into the Atlantic, the river Tamar marking its boundary with the rest of the country. Louisiana is swamp country: it too is almost an island, but in the Gulf of Mexico. Nowadays New Orleans is reached across Lake Pontchartrain by driving over the longest-spanning causeway in the world.

This comparative isolation gives each a sense of individuality. Terry Tomkins from the

AND LOUISIANA

Pilchard Works in Newlyn insists that he puts his nationality down as Cornish on forms. The Mappa Mundi, a map of the known world drawn up in the thirteenth century, shows Britain split into four parts: England, Scotland, Wales and Cornwall. Similarly, in Louisiana, New Orleans was colonised by the French and the Spanish, and even now many locals will acknowledge only very grudgingly that it is part of the United States.

With Terry Tomkin at the Newlyn Pilchard Works.

Cornwall and Louisiana also have their own sets of laws. The ancient Stannic Parliament in Cornwall had its own legislature which is no longer strictly adhered to, despite the efforts of its active supporters. When we visited we had to take a back road and sneak across the border, as the activists had closed Cornwall by demonstrating on the Tamar Bridge. For its part Louisiana has its own Napoleonic laws, that are still in force today. These include free crossing at certain bridges and particular ways of dividing lands and properties during a divorce.

In the course of our travels, we discovered one other very physical historical link. When the Arcadians were thrown out of Canada by the English (incidentally at about the same time as the Highlands of Scotland were being cleared) they did not head straight for Louisiana, as most thought, but were actually held in warehouses in the south of England until it could be decided what to do with them; some of those warehouses were of course in Cornwall. These folks are now called Cajuns – which is a simple corruption of the word Arcadian. They settled in the swamps of Louisiana because the Spanish governors of the time didn't want them in the cities. It was in these swamps that they met up with native Americans, who showed them the delights of swamp food and new herbs.

RIGHT: On board Cyrus Blanchard's shrimp boat, the 'Wild Turkey', in Louisiana.

BELOW: At Geevor Tin Mine with Johnny Johnson, ex-miner and guide.

'gator **gumbo**

Gumbo is the traditional swamp soup, and in Louisiana we use what we can find in the swamp. This time we had 'gator, but you could try frogs' legs, crawfish, shrimp, chicken, well let's face it, anything! The andouille sausage is made from chopped ham and heavily smoked, but any sausage that won't break into bits when simmered will do.

SERVES 16

- 250 ml (8 fl oz) oil
- 900 g (2 lb) 'gator or chicken, boned and cut up
- 675 g (1½ lb) andouille sausage
- 115g (4 oz) flour
- 8 medium onions, chopped
- 2 large sticks celery, chopped
- 450 g (1 lb) green peppers, deseeded and chopped
- 1 tbsp chopped garlic
- 2 litres (3½ pints) stock
- Joe's Stuff seasoning (or any premixed Creole seasoning blend)
- 225 g (8 oz) spring onions, chopped
- salt and freshly ground black pepper
- cooked rice or French bread, to serve
- *filé powder (optional), to serve

Heat a little oil in a large casserole over medium heat; season and brown the meat. Add the sausage and sauté with the meat. Remove both from the pot.

In the same casserole, make a roux with equal parts of oil and flour to the desired colour. Add the onions, celery and green pepper. Add the garlic and stir continuously.

When the vegetables are tender, return the meat and sausage to the casserole and cook, stirring frequently. Gradually stir in the stock and bring to the boil. Reduce the heat to a simmer and cook for 1 hour or more. Season with Joe's Stuff seasoning.

About 10 minutes before serving, add the spring onions. Serve over rice or with French bread.

*Filé powder is a fine green powder of young, dried, ground sassafras leaves, used in gumbo for flavour and thickening. It may be placed on the table to add to gumbo as desired. ¼ to ½ tsp per serving is recommended.

KB

oyster and artichoke soup

The key to cream soups is the one-to-one ratio of cream to stock. Some of my friends prefer their oysters very lightly poached. If you do too, you could try cooking them for just 1 minute.

SERVES 6–8

675 g (1½ lb) Jerusalem artichokes, quartered
1 litre (1¾ pints) strong chicken stock, or chicken stock substitute (see Note)
75 g (3 oz) spring onions, chopped
6 tsp thyme leaves
50 g (2 oz) butter, melted
5 tbsp flour
1 litre (1¾ pints) whipping cream
2 doz oysters
salt and cayenne pepper
75 g (3 oz) spring onions, chopped, to garnish
1 tbsp chopped parsley, to garnish

Place the artichokes, stock, spring onions, thyme and salt and cayenne pepper to taste in a large saucepan and bring to the boil. Reduce to a simmer and simmer for 12 minutes.

Combine the butter and flour for a light roux and add to the simmering soup. Stir in the whipping cream and simmer for 10 minutes.

Add the oysters and simmer for 5 more minutes. Serve garnished with chopped spring onions and parsley.

Note: The chicken stock substitute can be made from liquid from the oysters or the artichokes.

KB

fish **soup**

Although this is a soup, it can be served as a main course as it really is filling enough to make a meal in itself. It is ideal for supper parties when catching up with old friends; I love to serve it in rustic bowls, accompanied by a good selection of cheeses and a bottle of fine wine.

SERVES 4

175 g (6 oz) white onions, finely chopped
175 g (6 oz) white leeks, shredded
115 g (4 oz) fennel bulb, shredded
450 g (1 lb) firm white fish on the bone
1.75 litres (3 pints) fish stock
300 ml (½ pint) dry white wine
120 ml (4 fl oz) vermouth
juice of 1 lemon
2 tbsp olive oil
3 cloves garlic, crushed
1 tbsp fresh dill, chopped
2 tbsp chopped parsley
1 bay leaf
75 g (3 oz) white bread, crusts removed and cubed
50 g (2 oz) peeled prawns
50 g (2 oz) cooked mussels
75 g (3 oz) cooked clams
50 g (2 oz) cucumber, peeled and diced
225 g (8 oz) tomato flesh, diced
3 tbsp garlic mayonnaise
8 slices toasted French bread
salt and freshly ground black pepper

Place the white onions, leeks, fennel, fish, fish stock, white wine, vermouth and lemon juice in a pan and gently bring to the boil. The moment it bubbles, reduce the heat and simmer very gently for 20 minutes. Strain the liquid into a clean pan and remove the fish from the bones.

Heat the oil in a large pan, add the garlic, dill, parsley, bay leaf and bread. Cook gently for 3 minutes. Add the shellfish, cucumber, tomato flesh and fish stock. Bring slowly to the boil and add the cooked white fish. Check and, if necessary, adjust the seasoning.

To serve, spread the garlic mayonnaise over the toasted baguettes and serve them with the soup for floating on top.

KW

illustrated on previous pages

shrimp creole

The Creole sauce can be made ahead of company arriving. Heat the sauce and add the cooked shrimp when ready to eat. You can always substitute prawns for the shrimp, but it will not taste as meaty.

SERVES 8

115 g (4 oz) butter
1.5 kg (3 lb) peeled shrimp
8 tbsp flour
4 medium onions, chopped
1 large stick celery, chopped
225 g (8 oz) green pepper, deseeded and chopped
1 tbsp chopped garlic
750 ml (1¼ pints) chicken stock
400–450 g (14–16 oz) can tomato sauce
1 tbsp chopped thyme
1 tbsp chopped basil
3 bay leaves
1 tbsp brown sugar
4 thin slices lemon
Joe's Stuff seasoning (or any premixed Creole seasoning blend)
75 g (3 oz) chopped spring onions
50 g (2 oz) chopped parsley
cooked rice, to serve

Heat the butter in a large frying pan and sauté the shrimp for 2–3 minutes; transfer to a plate and set aside. Add the flour to the butter in the pan and stir over a medium heat until lightly browned.

Add the onions, celery, green pepper and garlic and sauté the vegetables until they begin to turn transparent. Add the stock, tomato sauce, thyme, basil, bay leaves, brown sugar, lemon slices, and Joe's Stuff seasoning. Simmer for about 10 minutes.

Add the spring onions, parsley and shrimp and simmer for another 5 minutes. Serve over rice.

KB

big kev's **barbecued shrimp**

In the States BBQ is a style of cooking rather than a method. These shrimps are done on the stove top in a BBQ sauce. The other trick to BBQ in the States is the way you serve it, never with a knife and fork, wear short sleeves and prepare to lick your elbows. If you can't get shrimps, try king prawns.

SERVES 4–6

300 ml (½ pint) beer
6–8 pints shrimp, in shell
4 tbsp Worcestershire sauce
1 tbsp fresh lemon juice
1 tsp garlic, very finely chopped
1 tsp all-purpose seasoning
225 g (8 oz) butter
bread, to serve

In a large frying pan, heat the beer over a medium high heat. Add the shrimp, Worcestershire sauce, lemon juice, garlic, and seasoning. Stir the shrimp in the mixture until they are cooked, about 5–6 minutes. Remove from the heat and stir in the butter until it melts. Serve with plenty of good bread to soak up the sauce.

KB

warm **monkfish** and **pilchard** tarts

The monkfish we saw being landed at Newlyn was fantastic and I couldn't resist using this. Unusually, I think the nearest American equivalent to monkfish (which they don't seem to have) is 'gator. I even thought that the 'gator tail looked like a monkfish tail. The pilchards are particular to Cornwall, we tried them in the Newlyn Pilchard Works pressed, filleted and stored in oil. A great taste that the Italians adore (and that's where most end up being shipped to). The nearest equivalent if you can't get the pilchards is anchovies or sardines.

SERVES 6

juice of 1 lemon
175 g (6 oz) skinned monkfish tail, diced
75 g (3 oz) spinach leaves
12 small cherry tomatoes, peeled
12 pitted black olives, halved
75 g (3 oz) salt-cured pilchard fillets
2 tbsp basil, chopped
2 eggs
175 ml (6 fl oz) whipping cream
2 tbsp grated Parmesan cheese
salt and freshly ground black pepper
salad, to serve

FOR THE PASTRY

250 g (9 oz) plain flour
pinch of salt
50 g (2 oz) butter, chilled and diced
25 g (1 oz) grated Parmesan cheese
1 tbsp chopped fresh sage
1½ tbsp very cold water
1 egg white

For the pastry, sift the flour and salt into a food processor and add the butter and Parmesan. Process until the mixture resembles fine breadcrumbs. Stir in the sage. Add the water until the mixture forms a ball. Transfer to a lightly floured surface and knead until smooth. Divide the pastry into 4 pieces and use to line 4 loose-bottomed 12 cm/4½ inch x 4 cm/½ inch tartlet tins. Refrigerate for 30 minutes.

Preheat the oven to 200°C/400°F/Gas 6. Line the pastry cases with greaseproof paper and baking beans, bake for 10 minutes. Remove the paper and beans and bake the cases for another 8 minutes. Finally, brush the base of each case with a small amount of the unbeaten egg white and return them to the oven for 1 minute. Remove from the oven and leave to cool.

Pour the lemon juice onto the monkfish and season with a little salt and pepper. Wilt the spinach by placing in a pan with a teaspoon of cold water and placing over a medium heat; drain and roughly chop.

Arrange the fish, spinach, tomatoes, olives and pilchard fillets in the tartlet cases; sprinkle with the chopped basil. Mix the eggs with the whipping cream and Parmesan. Add a little seasoning. Pour the mixture over the filling and bake in the oven for about 20 minutes or until just set in the centre and lightly browned. Carefully lift the tartlets out of the tins and serve warm with a little dressed salad.

KW

old-fashioned **tea-pickled pilchards**

This is a very old Cornish recipe that housewives would make for their fishermen husbands. It relies on the slow gentle heat from a cooling bake-house oven. After the morning baking the ovens were switched off until the evening. It was during this time the surrounding houses would bring their dishes of pilchards to be placed in the oven until it was time for the evening meal. Recently in Newlyn the pilchard works has tried to create this dish commercially, but the pilchards become so tender that it doesn't travel well.

SERVES 4–6

6 pilchards, gutted and descaled
coriander seeds
fennel seeds
whole green, red and black pepper
salt
1 tsp brown sugar
bay leaves
150 ml (¼ pint) strong tea
450 ml (¾ pint) malt vinegar

Place the pilchards head to tail in a 20 x 30 cm/8 x 12 inch ceramic dish. Sprinkle the coriander, fennel, peppers, salt and sugar over them and place several bay leaves across the top of the fish. Pour the tea and vinegar over to cover the fish. If the fish are not covered, make up some more liquid using tea and vinegar in a 1:3 ratio.

Cover the dish with greaseproof paper and then place a baking sheet over the top to act as a lid. Place in a preheated oven at 220°C/425°F/Gas 7 for 5 minutes or so until bubbling. Turn the oven down to 110°C/225°F/Gas ¼ and cook for 12 hours. The bones of the fish should be soft; serve cold with good bread and butter, but be careful handling the dish as the fish can easily break up, which spoils the look.

KW

wild **mushroom risotto**

This is a lovely starter and using dried porcini mushrooms gives the dish a more intense flavour.

SERVES 4

25 g (1 oz) dried porcini mushrooms
1 litre (1¾ pints) chicken stock
75 g (3 oz) butter
50 g (2 oz) shallots, finely diced
2 cloves garlic, crushed
225 g (8 oz) mixed fresh mushrooms, roughly chopped
275 g (10 oz) Arborio rice
4 tbsp sherry
50 g (2 oz) freshly grated Parmesan cheese
2 tbsp chopped fresh parsley
salt and freshly ground black pepper

Cover the dried porcini mushrooms with half the chicken stock and allow to soak for 30 minutes. Strain the liquid through a conical strainer back into the remainder of the chicken stock. Pick out the porcini mushrooms and roughly chop them.

Heat 50 g (2 oz) of the butter, add the shallots and cook without colouring; add the garlic, mushrooms and rice and stir to mix. Add the sherry and a ladleful of stock. Cook very gently over a low heat, gradually adding more stock, ladle by ladle, so that each addition of stock is absorbed before adding more. The risotto should retain a slight bite to each grain of rice, but at the same time have a creamy texture.

Once cooked, mix in the remaining butter, the grated Parmesan, chopped parsley and season to taste with salt and freshly ground black pepper.

The risotto looks beautiful when served in a deep, old fashioned soup dish.

KW

tuna an a bed of bubble and squeak with glazed red onions

Tuna is at its best when it is slightly undercooked and bubble and squeak is wonderful all the time.

SERVES 4

350 g (12 oz) potatoes for boiling, cubed
175 g (6 oz) cabbage, shredded
75 g (3 oz) carrots, chopped
115 g (4 oz) butter
8 tbsp olive oil
juice of 1 lemon
2 tbsp chopped fresh coriander
4 tuna steaks
175 g (6 oz) red onions, sliced
50 g (2 oz) soft muscovado sugar
pinch of allspice
2 tbsp chopped fresh mint
1 glass sherry
salt and freshly ground black pepper

Cook the potatoes, cabbage and carrots in separate pans of boiling salted water; drain and keep warm. Replace the potatoes in pan and place over a low heat for 1–2 minutes to dry. Mash the potatoes, add half the butter and 2 tbsp of the olive oil, then add the cabbage and carrots; mash together, season to taste and keep warm.

Prepare the marinade for the tuna; mix together 2 tbsp of olive oil, the lemon juice, coriander and seasoning. Pour over the tuna and leave for about 15 minutes.

Heat together the remaining butter and olive oil; add the sliced onions and cook gently for 10 minutes; add the sugar, allspice and increase the heat, allowing the sugar to caramelize. Stir in the mint and sherry, then cook for a further 2 minutes.

Divide the bubble and squeak mash into 4 equal portions and cook in a frying pan containing a little hot oil. Resist the temptation to turn them over too early, allow a crust to form on one side first.

Place a griddle pan over a high heat and add the tuna steaks. Cook for 2–3 minutes on each side or a little longer depending upon your preference. Place a portion of bubble and squeak on the plates, top with some glazed red onions and arrange thin slices of tuna steak on the top.

KW

red beans and rice

Red beans are traditionally served on Monday because this was wash day. The beans could cook on a low fire for hours without attention while the laundry was being done.

SERVES 6

450 g (1 lb) red kidney beans
1.5 litres (2½ pints) stock
3 tbsp vegetable oil
1 large onion, chopped
1 large stalk celery, chopped
225 g (8 oz) smoked sausage or ham chunks
2 tbsp chopped garlic
1 bay leaf
2 tbsp all-purpose seasoning
25 g (1 oz) chopped parsley
400 g (14 oz) rice, cooked, to serve

Soak the beans overnight. Drain the beans and place in a large saucepan with the stock over a low heat.

Coat a frying pan with oil and sauté the onion, celery and smoked sausage or ham chunks for 10 minutes.

Add the onion and sausage mixture to the beans and bring to a boil. Add the garlic, bay leaf, and all-purpose seasoning. Reduce to a simmer for 3 hours or until beans are creamy. Add more stock if necessary so the pan does not become dry. Remove the bay leaf, stir in the parsley and serve over cooked rice.

KB

jambalaya

Louisiana is one of America's biggest rice producers, so it's not surprising that dishes like Jambalaya are popular. A version of paella, it's really a question of catching anything you can and throwing it in – chicken, crayfish, shrimp, frog, whatever you've got.

SERVES 12

1 cooked chicken, boned and cut up
4 tbsp vegetable oil
675 g (1½ lb) spicy sausages
salt and freshly ground black pepper

FOR 'THE TRINITY'
8 medium onions, chopped
2 large sticks celery, chopped
450 g (1 lb) green pepper, deseeded and chopped
1 tbsp chopped garlic
800 g (1¾ lb) long grain rice
1.2 litres (2 pints) stock
2 heaped tsp Joe's Stuff seasoning
175 g (6 oz) chopped spring onions or tomatoes (optional)

Season the chicken and heat the oil in a large casserole over a medium-high heat; brown the chicken and then add the sausages to the casserole and sauté with the chicken. Remove both from the casserole.

For brown jambalaya either add 1 heaped tbsp brown sugar to the oil and caramelize, make a roux, or use gravy browning. For red jambalaya, add paprika for colour. If using gravy browning for brown jambalaya add 1 to 2 tbsp. For red jambalaya add approx 4 tbsp paprika, and you may want to use half stock and half tomato juice for the liquid.

Add the stock (or stock and tomato juice) to the casserole, add rice and return to boil. Cover and reduce the heat to a simmer. Cook for 20–25 minutes. After 10 minutes of cooking, remove cover and quickly turn rice from top to bottom completely. Season with Joe's Stuff or all-purpose seasoning. Add green onions and chopped tomatoes, if desired.

KB

chicken **étouffée**

This is a typical Cajun dish; étouffée translates as 'covered' or 'smothered in'. Cajun recipes can always be adjusted, for instance cooked shrimp can be substituted for the chicken (but it will take 5 minutes less cooking time).

SERVES 8

250 ml (8 fl oz) vegetable oil
115 g (4 oz) flour
2 tsp Joe's Stuff seasoning or any all-purpose seasoning
8 medium onions, chopped
4 medium sticks celery, chopped
1 large green pepper, deseeded and chopped
1 tbsp chopped garlic
475 ml (16 fl oz) chicken stock
900 g (2 lbs) diced chicken
chopped spring onions (optional)
chopped parsley (optional)
cooked rice, to serve

In a large pan, heat the oil and add the flour to make a dark roux, stirring constantly. Add seasoning blend to roux, along with onions, celery, green pepper, and garlic.

In another pan, heat the chicken stock until piping hot, stir in the roux gradually until blended well. Cook for 20 minutes over medium heat.

Add the chicken and cook an additional 10 minutes. If desired, chopped spring onions and parsley may be added 5 minutes before serving. Serve over rice.

KB

casserole of guinea fowl with tarragon dumplings

The rich flavours of this substantial dish make it one of my firm favourites. I love guinea fowl and the dumplings work well with any meat (you can change the herbs in them, too).

SERVES 4

- 1.75 litres (3 pints) chicken stock
- 115 g (4 oz) self-raising flour
- 50 g (2 oz) suet
- 3 tbsp chopped fresh tarragon
- 120 ml (4 fl oz) cold water
- 3 breasts of guinea fowl
- 1 tbsp paprika
- 2 tbsp plain flour
- 2 tbsp olive oil
- 115 g (4 oz) bacon, diced
- 50 g (2 oz) onion, finely diced
- 1 clove garlic, smashed
- 50 g (2 oz) leek, finely shredded
- 50 g (2 oz) celery, finely sliced
- 1 bouquet garni
- 1 tbsp grain mustard
- 50 ml (2 fl oz) whipping cream
- 1 egg yolk
- salt and freshly ground black pepper
- sprig of tarragon, to garnish

Bring a pan containing 1 litre (1¾ pints) of the chicken stock to the boil and then simmer.

Mix together the self-raising flour, suet, tarragon and salt and pepper. Make a well in the centre of the mixture, add the water and draw together to form a dough. Remove the dough from the bowl and gently knead, to ensure that all the ingredients are thoroughly mixed together. If the dough feels excessively sticky, dust with a little flour. Divide the dough into 20 small balls; place in the hot chicken stock and cook for 10–12 minutes.

Cut the guinea fowl into 5 cm/2 inch pieces. Mix the paprika and plain flour together and lightly dust the meat, so that there is a thin coating on each piece.

Heat the remaining 750 ml (1¼ pints) chicken stock. Heat the oil in a large casserole, add the guinea fowl and cook until lightly coloured. Add the bacon, cook for a further minute. Add the onion, garlic, leek and celery to the casserole, gently stir and allow to cook for a minute and then pour in the remaining chicken stock. Add the bouquet garni and season lightly with a salt and pepper. Cover and cook for 8–10 minutes, until the meat is cooked and the vegetables are tender.

Mix together the mustard, cream and egg yolk. Remove and discard the bouquet garni and add a little of the casserole stock to the cream mixture. Remove the casserole from the heat and slowly pour the cream mixture into the casserole, stirring continuously. Drain the dumplings and spoon the guinea fowl and vegetables into a large soup dish. Arrange the dumplings around the dish and garnish with a sprig of tarragon.

KW

cornish **saffron cake** with summer berry jam

The saffron cake was derived in Cornwall during the period when locally mined tin was traded for saffron, thus making this exotic ingredient available to local people. This fairly heavy cake is more aptly described as tea bread and is complemented by my favourite low-sugar summer berry jam.

SERVES 4–6 (AT LEAST!)

FOR THE SAFFRON CAKE
pinch of saffron
2 tbsp warm water
450 g (1 lb) plain white flour
30 g (1 oz) dried yeast
90 g (3½ oz) sugar
1 tsp mixed spice
pinch of salt
175 g (6 oz) unsalted butter, chilled and cubed
50 g (2 oz) raisins
25 g (1 oz) sultanas
25 g (1 oz) glacé cherries
25 g (1 oz) flaked almonds
25 g (1 oz) walnuts
zest of 1 orange
200 ml (7 fl oz) warm milk

FOR THE SUMMER BERRY JAM
225 g (8 oz) strawberries
115 g (4 oz) raspberries
115 g (4 oz) blackcurrants
175 g (6 oz) sugar
1 tbsp water

Place the saffron into warm water and leave to soak for at least 2 hours. Sieve the flour into a bowl, add the yeast, sugar, mixed spice and salt. Mix all the ingredients together.

Lightly rub the butter into the mixture and then add the dried fruit, nuts and orange zest. Pour in the warm milk and saffron. Mix to form a dough and cover with a wet cloth. Leave in a warm place until the dough doubles in size.

Knock the dough back down and mould into a 23 x 13 cm/ 9 x 5 inch bread tin. Leave to rise for 30–40 minutes.

Bake in a preheated oven at 190°C/375°F/Gas 5 for 30–40 minutes, remove and cool.

Make the summer berry jam; gently rinse the fruits, removing stalks etc. Place the blackcurrants in a pan with the water and simmer for 5 minutes or until the fruit is tender. Add the other fruits and simmer until they soften, about 5 minutes.

Remove the pan from the heat and gently stir in the sugar, making sure that it dissolves. Return to the heat and boil rapidly, for about 10 minutes until the setting point is reached. Spoon into warm jars, allow to cool and refrigerate.

KW

pralines

Creole confections occupy a unique position in the United States. The most popular of these is the praline. Pralines derive their name from Marshal Luplesis-Praslin (1598–1695) and his butler's recipe for almonds coated in sugar, used as a digestive aid. When Louisiana was settled by French colonists, native pecans were substituted for almonds.

No lengths were spared by the Creoles to achieve perfection in candy making. Along with their vast collection of Creole recipes, cooks had their own secret method for making the best pralines, which they guarded carefully and handed down from generation to generation.

Today pralines are as many and varied as they were in the very beginning. We hope your memories of New Orleans are as sweet as pralines!

MAKES 25–30

275 g (10 oz) sugar
175 g (6 oz) light brown sugar, packed
120 ml (4 fl oz) milk
75 g (3 oz) butter
250 g (9 oz) pecans (roasted if you like)
1 tsp vanilla essence

Combine all ingredients in a saucepan over a medium heat and bring to a 'softball' stage (119°C/238°F), stirring constantly. (Test by placing a spoonful in a glass of water; it should stick to the side.) Remove from the heat.

Stir until the mixture thickens, becomes creamy and cloudy, and pecans stay suspended in the mixture. Spoon out onto buttered waxed paper, aluminium foil or greaseproof paper and allow to cool. (When using waxed paper, be sure to protect with newspaper underneath, as hot wax will transfer to worktop or table.)

Note: to roast pecans, bake them on a baking sheet at 140°C/275°F/Gas 1 for 20–25 minutes, until slightly browned and fragrant.

KB

crème brûlée

Just look at the ingredients and you know it's good. Stand back from the stove and put down the cream if you are worried about your diet.

SERVES 6

75 g (3 oz) sugar
8 large egg yolks
475 ml (16 fl oz) whipping cream
1 tbsp vanilla
sugar, for topping

In a bowl, beat the sugar and egg yolks until the sugar has dissolved. Add the whipping cream and vanilla, mixing until well blended. Pour the mixture through a strainer into a glass measuring jug. This will keep the mixture smooth and free of lumps.

Pour the mixture into individual ramekins and place in a baking tin. Fill the baking tin with warm water halfway up the side of the ramekins. Cover with foil and bake in a preheated oven at 150°C/300°F/Gas 2 for 40–50 minutes. Take the tin from the oven and allow to cool. Place the ramekins in the refrigerator to chill.

To serve, sprinkle 2 tsp sugar on the top of each ramekin and place under the hot grill to melt the sugar. The sugar can also be caramelized with a hand-held torch.

KB

parmesan and thyme crumpets

Crumpets have a strong foothold in British culture, they conjure up childhood images of toasting forks, log fires and crisp autumnal days. However by incorporating Parmesan and thyme into the recipe, the crumpet is transformed into an ideal Euro snack and is a smashing base upon which to present many more complex dishes.

MAKES 20

350 g (12 oz) plain flour
pinch of salt
75 g (3 oz) grated Parmesan cheese
15 g (½ oz) fresh yeast
pinch of caster sugar
600 ml (1 pint) lukewarm water
1 tbsp fresh thyme leaves

Sieve together the flour and salt. Add the grated Parmesan and mix through. Dilute the yeast in a small bowl with 4 tbsp of water and a pinch of caster sugar. Slowly add 450 ml (¾ pint) of the warm water to the flour, whisking to a batter and then add the thyme and diluted yeast.

Cover with a damp cloth and leave in a warm place until it has risen by at least one third. The batter should have a pouring consistency, if necessary add a little of the remaining water.

For best results pour the batter into greased crumpet rings which are sitting in a lightly greased frying pan over a low heat (be sure to only half fill the rings). Once the top of the crumpets show small holes beginning to appear, carefully turn the crumpets over and cook for a further minute or so until golden brown.

Serve toasted, heavily laden with butter. Scrambled eggs with a little smoked salmon running through is a wonderful accompaniment.

KW

bananas foster

New Orleans was a major port for importing bananas. This dish was invented by chef Owen Brennan for his friend Foster, and helped use up some of those bananas. The flame is for presentation. Don't burn down the house to impress your friends. It tastes just as good not flamed.

SERVES 4

50 g (2 oz) butter
225 g (8 oz) dark brown sugar
2 bananas
50 ml (2 fl oz) banana liqueur
120 ml (4 fl oz) dark rum
ground cinnamon
ice cream, to serve

In a frying pan, melt the butter and add the brown sugar to form a creamy paste. Allow the mixture to caramelize over a medium heat for about 5 minutes.

Slice the bananas lengthwise and then chop each piece in half through the middle. Stir in the bananas, banana liqueur and rum. Heat and ignite. Agitate to keep flame burning and add a few pinches of cinnamon (voodoo magic!) to the flame.

Let the flame go out and serve over ice cream.

KB

warm **almond** and **pear tart** served with clotted cream

A combination of almonds and pears, served warm in this tart, gives a combination of flavours and texture which satisfies something deep inside my soul (the clotted cream is optional).

SERVES 4

350 g (12 oz) plain flour, sifted
350 g (12 oz) unsalted butter, diced
pinch of salt
115 g (4 oz) icing sugar, sifted
zest of ½ lemon
2 eggs
1 star anise
juice of 1 orange
½ stick cinnamon
3 cloves
4 ripe pears, peeled, cored and quartered
115 g (4 oz) ground almonds
115 g (4 oz) caster sugar
3 tbsp strawberry jam
icing sugar and cocoa powder, to decorate
clotted cream (optional), to serve

Make the pastry: put the sifted flour into a bowl and place 225 g (8 oz) of the butter and a pinch of salt in the centre. Gently rub the butter into the flour, until the texture is sandy. Add the sifted icing sugar, lemon zest and 1 egg, and gently mix together to form a dough. Knead the dough very gently for a minute, until it becomes smooth. Cover and refrigerate for about 3 hours.

Roll out the pastry and line a deep 20 cm/8 inch baking tin. Cover with greaseproof paper and fill with baking beans. Bake blind in a preheated oven at 180°C/350°F/Gas 4 for 8–10 minutes. Remove from the oven and discard the beans and paper. Place the baking tin back in the oven for a further 4–6 minutes, then remove from the oven and allow to cool.

For the filling, place the star anise, orange juice, cinnamon and cloves in a pan, add the pears and gently poach until the pears are soft. Remove the pears from the cooking liquid and leave to cool.

Place the remaining butter, ground almonds and sugar in a food processor and blend until smooth; add the remaining egg and mix through.

Cover the base of the tart with strawberry jam, pour on the almond mixture and arrange the pears over the top. Bake in a preheated oven at 200°C/400°F/Gas 6 for 30–40 minutes, until cooked and golden brown.

Dust the top first with icing sugar, followed by a little cocoa powder and serve with clotted cream.

KW

pina colada bread pudding

Any type of bread can be used from doughnuts, Danish pastries, rolls, cinnamon rolls, fresh bread – you name it. Just place the bread in the paper bags to dry out. It is important that it is completely dry.

SERVES 16–20

275 g (10 oz) loaf stale French bread, crumbled
1 litre (1¾ pints) milk
200 g (14 oz) sugar
115 (4 oz) butter, melted
3 eggs
2 tsp vanilla essence
175 g (6 oz) crushed pineapple
75 g (3 oz) desiccated coconut
1 tsp cinnamon
1 tsp nutmeg

FOR THE SAUCE
115 g (4 oz) butter
375 g (10 oz) caster sugar
2 egg yolks
120 ml (4 fl oz) rum

Combine all the pudding ingredients; the mixture should be very moist but not too liquid. Pour into a buttered 23 x 30 cm/ 9 x 12 inch baking dish or larger. Place into non-preheated oven. Bake at 180°C/350°F/Gas 4 for about 1 hour 15 minutes, until top is golden brown.

Meanwhile, make the sauce; cream the butter and sugar over a medium heat until the butter is absorbed. Remove from the heat and blend in the egg yolks. Pour in the rum gradually to taste, stirring constantly. Sauce will thicken as it cools. Serve warm over the warm bread pudding.

Note: for a variety of sauces, just substitute your favourite fruit juice or liqueur to complement your bread pudding.

KB

cornish **apple** and **cinnamon** cake

This cake not only eats well, but it keeps well when stored in an airtight container. You can add a little lemon or orange zest to the topping ingredients if you prefer a sharper taste.

SERVES 6–8

FOR THE CAKE
175 g (6 oz) caster sugar
175 g (6 oz) unsalted butter
3 eggs, beaten
350 g (12 oz) self-raising flour
450 g (1 lb) English cooking apples, peeled and grated
225 g (8 oz) sultanas
finely grated zest of 1 lemon
1 tsp cinnamon

FOR THE TOPPING
150 g (5 oz) plain flour
50 g (2 oz) icing sugar
75 g (3 oz) butter, chilled and cut up

Beat the caster sugar and butter together until the mixture becomes smooth and creamy. Add the eggs a little at a time until they are incorporated. Then fold in the flour and add the grated apples, sultanas, lemon zest and cinnamon. Mix together and pour into a 23 cm/9 inch round, loose-bottomed cake tin.

Make the topping; sieve together the flour and icing sugar. Gently rub in the cold butter until the mixture has a sandy texture and cover the cake mix with the crumble topping.

Cook in a preheated oven at 180°C/350°F/Gas 4 for 16–18 minutes until firm and moist.

KW

YORKSHIRE

Buying chillies in Guadalajara's main market.

This is the story of the world's most common spice, the chilli, chili or pepper. The name varies, as does the strength.

The chilli was discovered for the western world in Mexico by the Conquistadors in the seventeenth century. It was traded into English ports, but the British knew it to be a member of the deadly nightshade family and so passed it on to other parts of the world such as India. It entered every kind of dish you could want to mention, its subtler and harsher flavours being discovered and experimented with. Eventually it returned to the UK in the 1960s when Indians were invited to come and live and work in Britain because of a labour shortage. Nowadays towns like Bradford, London and Birmingham have significant Indian populations and the chilli is available everywhere. Its flavour has migrated into many British dishes.

In Mexico the chilli's success was no less rampant. Pepper seeds have been found in archaeological remains dated to 7500 BC.

AND MEXICO

Today there are over 100 varieties ranging from the mildest bell pepper to the hottest habanero. Hot pepper sauces can be found on just about every table in the States. Eggs without chilli sauce would be unthinkable to most cowboys at breakfast. Nachos with chilli sauce and whole pickled chillies are consumed by the bucket load at movie theatres across America. Big Kevin eats enough chillies not to be bothered by their heat, but you might want to use milder ones or less of the hot ones in his recipes.

Making chilli lemonade, a 'hot' cold drink.

A jimador harvesting agave, used to make tequilla.

parsnip and smoked ham soup

Although the ingredients for this soup might appear heavy, the resulting dish is light with a lovely depth of flavour. A smaller quantity of this also makes a delightful sauce to accompany pork dishes.

SERVES 4

50 ml (2 fl oz) olive oil
75 g (3 oz) smoked bacon, diced
75 g (3 oz) onions, finely diced
2 cloves garlic, crushed
450 g (1 lb) parsnips, cored and chopped
½ tsp cumin
½ tsp turmeric
½ tsp chilli powder
115 g (4 oz) cooking apples, peeled, cored and chopped
750 ml (1¼ pints) chicken or vegetable stock
300 ml (½ pint) whipping cream
salt and freshly ground black pepper
garlic croûtons or warm granary bread, to serve

Heat the oil in a deep saucepan; add the diced bacon, onion, garlic, parsnips and cook gently for 5–8 minutes without colouring. Add the spices and chopped apples and stir thoroughly.

Pour on the stock and bring to the boil. Reduce the heat, cover and allow to simmer for 30–40 minutes until the parsnips are cooked. Leave the soup to cool and then transfer to a blender and blend to a purée. Return the soup to the pan, add the cream, season with salt and pepper and return to the boil.

To serve, pour the soup into a large soup bowl and top with garlic croûtons or serve with warm granary bread.

KW

avocado and black bean **salsa**

If I don't eat this in one sitting, I use it as a topping for baked chicken, and I know what you're saying – that can't be very often. If you can't get black beans, use black-eyed beans instead.

SERVES 2

1 firm-ripe avocado, finely chopped
½ red onion, finely chopped
1 tomato, finely chopped
65 g (2½ oz) canned black beans, rinsed and drained
2 tbsp fresh lime juice
1 tsp olive oil
salt
tortilla chips or crisps, to serve

In a bowl, mix together the avocado, onion and tomato with the beans, lime juice, oil and salt to taste. Serve the salsa with tortilla chips or crisps.

KB

quick fry **whitebait**

In Chapulla, Mexico, every street stand sells these to snack on as you stroll by the edge of the lake.

SERVES 4–6

115 g (4 oz) flour
3 tbsp ground red chilli
3 tbsp freshly ground black pepper
3 tbsp salt
250 ml (8 fl oz) milk
1 large egg, beaten
2 limes, cut into quarters
450–900 g (1–2 lb) whitebait
vegetable oil, for deep frying

In a bowl, season the flour with half of the red chilli, black pepper and salt.

In another bowl, mix the milk and egg.

Squeeze juice from half the lime pieces over the whitebait, then sprinkle a pinch of red chilli, black pepper and salt over the top. Place some of the whitebait in the milk mixture, then in the seasoned flour to coat.

Heat the oil in a heavy pan until very hot. Shake any excess coating off the whitebait and drop in the hot oil. Fry for 2 minutes until crisp. Drain on kitchen paper, sprinkle with a pinch of seasoning and a squeeze of lime. Repeat until all the whitebait are cooked.

Serve when cool enough to eat.

KB

jicama **slaw**

I can guarantee once you start to use jicama it will always be on your grocery list. Jicama is a root vegetable from Central America, with a thin brown skin and crisp, juicy white flesh. One of my favourite ways to eat it is julienned and sprinkled lightly with red pepper.

SERVES 4

- 450 g (1 lb) jicama*, peeled and grated
- 1 large carrot, peeled and grated
- 3 tbsp lime juice
- 2 tbsp mayonnaise
- 1 tbsp chopped fresh coriander
- 1 tsp ground cumin
- ½ tsp Tabasco sauce
- salt and freshly ground black pepper

In a large bowl, combine jicama, carrot, lime juice, mayonnaise, coriander, cumin and Tabasco sauce. Season with salt and pepper then cover and refrigerate for 1 hour.

* If you cannot get jicama, use seeded cucumber instead.

KB

red pepper and artichoke fritatta

I like to serve this as a side dish with a salad. It's a bit like a crustless quiche.

SERVES 4

- 2 tsp olive oil
- 1 red pepper, deseeded and diced
- 1 tbsp very finely chopped garlic
- ¼ tsp crushed red pepper
- 4 large eggs
- 2 egg whites
- 185 g (6½ oz) artichoke hearts, chopped
- 25 g (1 oz) grated Parmesan cheese
- 1 tsp chopped fresh oregano
- ½ tsp salt
- ¼ tsp freshly ground black pepper

In a non-stick frying pan, heat 1 tsp of the oil and sauté the red pepper until tender. Add the garlic and crushed pepper, stirring for another minute. Transfer the garlic and pepper mixture to a bowl and wipe the pan clean.

In another bowl, mix the eggs and egg whites, and stir in the artichokes, pepper mixture, Parmesan, oregano, salt and pepper.

Add 1 tsp oil to the clean pan and heat. Pour in the mixture, cooking until the underside is lightly browned. Protect the pan handle with foil if necessary and place the pan under the grill; cook until the eggs are set, about 1 minute. Cut into wedges and serve.

KB

illustrated on previous pages

green chilli **cheesecake**

Sounds unusual but if you pick your chillies well then the balance of this dish can be perfect. The cheesecake takes away a lot of the fire from the chilli and gives you that great pepper taste. It's quite a rich dish so don't serve much for a starter. You can also add some dried sausage to ring the changes.

SERVES 8

FOR THE CRUST

- 115 g (4 oz) blue cornmeal
- 50 g (2 oz) unsalted butter, melted
- 50 ml (2 fl oz) boiling water

FOR THE FILLING

- 8 fresh green chillies
- 350 ml (12 fl oz) sour cream
- 2 large eggs
- 25 g (1 oz) unsalted butter
- 450 g (1 lb) cream cheese, softened
- 115 g (4 oz) Monterey Jack cheese, grated
- 175 g (6 oz) Cheddar cheese, grated
- 1 tbsp very finely chopped dill leaves
- 15 g (½ oz) fresh coriander, chopped
- salt

Make the crust; place the cornmeal in a bowl, and stir in the melted butter and water. Press the mixture onto the bottom of a 25 cm/10 inch springform pan.

Preheat the grill. Place the chillies on the rack of the grill pan, and grill 5 cm/2 inches away from the heat. Turn them frequently until the skins are charred and blistered, 5–6 minutes. Place the chillies in a bowl and cover until cool enough to handle, then peel them. Discard the seeds and finely chop the chillies. Remember to wash your hands thoroughly after handling the chillies.

In a food processor, blend the sour cream and eggs. Add the butter and cream cheese, blending until smooth. Place the mixture in a bowl and add the two cheeses, the dill, coriander and salt to taste.

Pour the filling into the pie crust and bake in a preheated oven at 160°C/325°F/ Gas 3 for 45 minutes or until centre is set. Cool the cheesecake in the pan on a rack before cutting.

KB

chilli salmon cakes on a warm potato salad

This tasty meal will revive even the most jaded palate, so put some spice in your life!

SERVES 6

3 tbsp grated fresh ginger root
350 g (12 oz) salmon fillets
juice of 2 limes
75 g (3 oz) spring onions, finely diced
3 cloves garlic, smashed
4 red chillies, deseeded and finely diced
4 tbsp fresh coriander, chopped
1 tbsp olive oil
2 tbsp anchovy essence
275 g (10 oz) dried breadcrumbs
115 g (4 oz) plain flour
3 eggs, beaten
675 g (1½ lb) new potatoes
1 bunch lemon mint
grated zest of ½ lemon
90 ml (3 fl oz) olive oil
juice of 1 lemon
2 tbsp snipped chives
8 tbsp crème fraîche
vegetable oil, for frying
salt and freshly ground black pepper
6 coriander leaves, to garnish

Spread the grated ginger over the salmon fillets, season with salt and freshly ground black pepper and place in a steamer. Sprinkle the salmon with the lime juice and steam until cooked. If you don't have a steamer then use a microwave or put the fish on a plate, cover with clear film or foil and place the plate on top of a pan containing boiling water.

Allow the salmon to cool, transfer to a bowl and break up with a fork. Add the spring onion, garlic, chillies, coriander, 1 tbsp olive oil and anchovy essence and mix together with the salmon. Season to taste. Mix in 175 g (6 oz) of the breadcrumbs, ensuring that all the ingredients are well incorporated.

Put the flour, eggs and remaining breadcrumbs into three separate dishes. Divide the salmon mixture into 12 and dip each portion into the flour, then the egg and finally coat with breadcrumbs. Using a palette knife, gently shape into round cakes, ensuring that each cake is coated with crumbs.

Cook the new potatoes in a pan of boiling salted water with lots of lemon mint. Drain well and break the potatoes lightly, using a fork. Add the 90 ml (3 fl oz) olive oil, lemon zest, half the lemon juice, snipped chives and 5 tbsp of the crème fraîche. Season with salt and pepper, cover and keep warm. Mix the remaining 3 tbsp of crème fraîche with the remaining lemon juice and keep refrigerated until needed.

Heat a little vegetable oil in a frying pan and cook the salmon until golden brown. To serve, gently press a portion of the warm potato salad into a 10 cm/4 inch ring mould or use a palette knife to form a neat circle about 3 cm/1¼ inches high on the centre of the plate. Place 2 salmon cakes on top of the salad and garnish with ½ tbsp of the lemon crème fraîche and a coriander leaf.

KW

pepper onion **quesadillas** with salsa

I have made this with as many as seven different peppers – the more the merrier!

SERVES 4

225 g (8 oz) red pepper, deseeded and diced
225 g (8 oz) yellow pepper, deseeded and diced
2 jalapeño chillies, deseeded and diced
115 g (4 oz) chopped sweet onion
½ tsp salt
½ tsp ground cumin
¼ tsp freshly ground black pepper
vegetable oil, for frying
8 corn tortillas
115 g (4 oz) Monterey Jack cheese, grated

FOR THE SALSA
4 medium tomatoes, diced
115 g (4 oz) jicama*, peeled and diced
115 g (4 oz) onion, diced
150 g (5 oz) radishes, diced
25 g (1 oz) cucumber, deseeded and diced
½ tsp salt
4 mint leaves, chopped
2 tbsp chopped fresh coriander
1 jalapeño chilli, deseeded and diced
4 tbsp orange juice
2 tbsp lime juice

Make the salsa; place all the ingredients in a large bowl and toss gently. Cover and refrigerate until ready to serve.

In a bowl, combine the peppers, chillies, onion, salt, cumin and black pepper.

Lightly coat a large pan with oil and place over a medium heat. Place 1 tortilla in the pan and top with a quarter of the pepper mixture then sprinkle with a quarter of the cheese. Spread over the tortilla and place another tortilla on top.

Cook 2 minutes on each side, pressing down with a spatula, until golden brown. Keep the quesadilla warm and repeat with the remaining tortillas and pepper mixture. Top with the salsa and serve.

*If you cannot find jicama, use seeded cucumber instead.

KB

toasted monkfish with a rhubarb sauce

Rhubarb is a very British ingredient, used to accompany fish many years ago.

SERVES 4

500 g (1¼ lb) monkfish tail fillets
75 g (3 oz) white breadcrumbs
25 g (1 oz) chopped parsley
25 g (1 oz) sesame seeds
50 g (2 oz) Dijon mustard
120 ml (4 fl oz) water
50 g (2 oz) granulated sugar
225 g (8 oz) rhubarb, trimmed
175 ml (6 fl oz) fish stock
75 g (3 oz) unsalted butter, chilled and cubed
juice of ½ lemon
vegetable oil, for frying
4 portions young spinach leaves
50 g (2 oz) pine kernels
chives, to garnish
salt and freshly ground black pepper

Cut the monkfish into 12 equal slices. Mix the breadcrumbs with the parsley and sesame seeds. Season the fish and brush a little Dijon mustard over each side. Dip the fish in the breadcrumbs so that each side is coated and place to one side.

Place the water in a pan, add the sugar and bring to the boil. Simmer until the mixture becomes syrupy, but not coloured.

Cut the rhubarb into 4 cm/1½ inch pieces, keeping 40 pieces for garnish. To prepare the rhubarb garnish, cook the 40 pieces in the sugar syrup until soft, but ensuring they retain their shape, then remove the pieces from the syrup and keep to one side. Cook the rest of the rhubarb in the syrup; when cooked, remove from the liquid and sieve to produce a purée.

Place the fish stock over a high heat and reduce until it becomes thick and syrupy; add the rhubarb purée and bring back to the boil for 30 seconds, then remove from the heat completely. Quickly whisk in the chilled butter, check and adjust seasoning with salt, pepper and lemon juice. Transfer the sauce to a jug, cover and keep warm, but do not reheat.

Cook the monkfish in a frying pan with a little oil for about 1 minute each side – ideally it should be slightly undercooked. Remove from the pan, cover and keep warm. Add the pine kernels to the frying pan, cook for 30 seconds and then add the spinach; season with salt and freshly ground black pepper and allow the spinach to wilt.

To serve, place a high portion of the spinach on each plate, top with the monkfish slices and drizzle the rhubarb sauce around the outside. Then assemble the rhubarb garnish pieces on top of the monkfish. Finally, criss-cross small pieces of chives around the outside of the dish.

KW

green **chilli verde**

They reckon that pumpkins and squashes were around in Mexico well before 7000 BC. This recipe uses the shell, as a serving pot, as well as the flesh.

SERVES 4–6

3 tbsp vegetable oil
900 g (2 lb) chicken, diced
450 g (1 lb) lean minced pork
6 cloves garlic, very finely chopped
1.5 kg (3–3½ lb) canned tomatoes
50 g (2 oz) chopped parsley
175 g (6 oz) green chillies (fresh or canned), deseeded and chopped
2 tsp ground cumin
2 tsp oregano
1 tsp chilli powder
50 ml (2 fl oz) lemon juice
50 ml (2 fl oz) lime juice
175 ml (6 fl oz) beef stock
1 large pumpkin
1 small sugar pumpkin
dash of Tabasco sauce
salt and freshly ground black pepper
1 bunch spring onions, chopped, to garnish
sour cream, to serve

In a large casserole, heat the oil and brown the chicken and pork. Add the garlic and cook for 5 minutes.

Add the tomatoes and their juice and break them up with the back of a spoon. Add the parsley, chillies, cumin, oregano, chilli powder, lemon and lime juice and beef stock. Cook in the casserole, covered, over a low heat for at least 1 hour, stirring occasionally, and adding more stock if necessary.

Perpare the pumpkins; cut the top from the large pumpkin, about a third of the way down. Scoop out the seeds and stringy fibres, then put pumpkin on a sturdy ovenproof dish and warm it slowly in the oven at 120°C/250°F/Gas 1–2 for 15 minutes, to warm it slightly. Cut the sugar pumpkin into quarters, remove the seeds and stringy fibre. Peel off the outer rind with a sharp knife and cut the pumpkin flesh into 2.5 cm/1 inch cubes.

Add the cubed pumpkin to the casserole and simmer, uncovered, for 15 minutes. Season and add the Tabasco sauce.

Place the contents of the casserole in the large pumpkin shell and bake for 15 minutes. Garnish with spring onions and serve straight from the shell, with sour cream and Indian blue Cornbread (see p. 80).

KB

indian blue **cornbread**

This is the perfect thing to serve with Green Chilli Verde (see previous page). If you cannot get blue corn, don't worry: any colour will do for taste, if not for looks.

SERVES 8

- 2 tbsp lard or bacon fat
- 1 small onion, very finely chopped
- 115 g (4 oz) blue, white or yellow cornmeal
- 115 g (4 oz) unbleached flour
- 1 tsp salt
- 1 tbsp baking powder
- 250 ml (8 fl oz) milk
- 2 eggs, beaten
- 50–115 g (2–4 oz) cheese, diced
- 115 g (4 oz) pork crackling or 75 g (3 oz) crumbled, cooked bacon

Heat the lard or bacon fat in a 20 cm/8 inch ovenproof frying pan over a medium heat, and sauté the onion.

Mix together the cornmeal, flour, salt and baking powder in a bowl. Add the onion and all the remaining ingredients, and pour the mixture into the hot frying pan. Bake in a preheated oven at 230°C/450°F/Gas 8 for 20–25 minutes. Cut into wedges and serve with the Green Chilli Verde.

KB

Jamil's **kurai chicken**

The recipe for this traditional chicken curry has been in Jamil's family for generations. Not only is this the award-winning chef's signature dish, but it is also his favourite food! The use of so many whole spices gives this dish real complexity and flavour. If you like curry, this is Nirvana.

SERVES 4

olive oil, for frying
1 medium onion, sliced
8 tomatoes, quartered
1 stick cinnamon
6 bay leaves
6 whole cardamom pods
6 whole green cardamom pods
4 cloves garlic, sliced
2.5 cm/1 inch square fresh ginger root, sliced
12 whole cloves
1 heaped tsp chilli powder
1 heaped tsp paprika
1 heaped tsp turmeric
1 green pepper, sliced
4 green chillies, split
1 tsp salt
450 g (1 lb) chicken, cubed
1 large bunch fresh coriander

Heat some olive oil in a wide heavy-bottomed sauté or frying pan. Fry the sliced onion and half of the tomatoes until the onion starts to brown.

Add the cinnamon, bay leaves, cardamom pods and green cardamom pods. Cook for a minute to release the flavour, then toss in the sliced garlic and ginger for a further minute's cooking. Place in the cloves and enough water to produce a thin paste. Make sure you scrape all the spices off the bottom of the pan and stir them into the gravy.

Add the chilli powder, paprika, and turmeric, followed by the sliced green pepper and the fresh chillies. Cook for a further minute.

Add the remaining tomatoes and the salt. Cook for a further minute. Add the cubed chicken and enough water to cover the ingredients. Then cover the pan and leave to simmer for 15 minutes.

Prior to serving, chop the coriander and stir a large handful into the curry. Serve immediately.

KW

pork meatballs with coriander couscous

The inspiration for this dish came from the Indian and Pakistan communities in Yorkshire. Allow the meat time to absorb the flavours from the sauce.

SERVES 4

FOR THE COUSCOUS
115 g (4 oz) couscous
350 ml (12 fl oz) vegetable stock, hot
50 ml (2 fl oz) olive oil
bunch of fresh coriander, chopped
3 red and 3 green chillies, deseeded and finely chopped
2 tsp chilli oil

FOR THE MEATBALLS
175 g (6 oz) onion, finely chopped
2 cloves garlic, crushed
450 g (1 lb) minced lean pork
2 egg yolks
1 tsp cinnamon
2 tsp chilli powder
2 tsp paprika
1 tsp cumin seeds
vegetable oil, for frying
salt and pepper

FOR THE SAUCE
50 ml (2 fl oz) olive oil
115 g (4 oz) onion, finely chopped
3 cloves garlic, crushed
675 g (1½ lb) over-ripe tomatoes, peeled, deseeded and chopped
2 tbsp sun-dried tomato purée
2 glasses dry white wine
½ tsp Tabasco sauce
½ tsp Worcestershire sauce
pinch of caster sugar

To make the couscous, place the couscous in a bowl and pour the vegetable stock over it, season with salt and mix in the olive oil. Allow to stand for 10 minutes and then add the chopped coriander, red and green chillies and chilli oil and cover with clear film.

To make the meatballs, mix together the onion, garlic and minced pork. Add the egg yolks, cinnamon, chilli powder and paprika. Crush the cumin seeds in the palm of your hand prior to sprinkling them into the mixture and season with salt and pepper. Divide the mixture into 20 small meatballs and gently cook in a frying pan containing hot oil, turning frequently.

To prepare the sauce, heat the olive oil and cook the onion and garlic, add the chopped tomatoes and cook for 3–4 minutes. Add the sun-dried tomato purée, white wine, Tabasco and Worcestershire sauce, season with salt, pepper and a pinch of caster sugar.

To serve, microwave the couscous on high for 45 seconds, spoon into tightly buttered ramekins or dariole moulds and unmould onto the centre of a serving plate. Surround the couscous with 5 meatballs and top each one with tomato sauce.

KW

traditional hand-raised **pork pie**

Eat this and you'll never buy another supermarket pork pie in your life. This is the real thing, moist, filling and delicious. It is also pretty simple to make, if a little bit fiddly. One tip, make sure you use good pork. Cheap fatty cuts will result in a cheap fatty pie.

SERVES 6

FOR THE CRUST
225 g (8 oz) lard
450 g (1 lb) of strong white flour
pinch of salt

FOR THE FILLING
450 g (1 lb) good quality minced pork
1 tsp fresh sage
1 tsp each salt and freshly ground black pepper

FOR THE JELLY
600 ml (1 pint) well-flavoured meat stock

FOR THE GLAZE
1 beaten egg

Melt the lard, then add it to the flour and salt and mix into a dough. Turn the dough out onto a floured surface and knead for a few moments, leave aside some dough for the lid. Flatten the remaining dough into a saucer around 15 cm/6 inches across. Make sure the disc of dough is thicker at the sides than in the middle.

Mix the minced pork together with the sage, salt and pepper and roll into a ball. Place the ball of pork on the dough and start to build the dough into walls until it surrounds the pork. When this is complete, dampen the lid with egg and place the lid, egg side down, on top of the pie. With a fork, carefully press the lid and the sides together to seal the pie closed. Then prick a large hole in the centre of the lid. Coat the entire pie in a glaze of beaten egg.

Bake the pie in a preheated oven at 200°C/400°F/Gas 6 for about 20 minutes until golden brown.

While the pie is cooking, reduce the stock to about a third. It should be slightly thick and jelly like. Remove the pie from the oven and, if necessary, re-open the hole in the top which may have sealed over during cooking. Pour the jelly stock into the hole and leave the pie to stand for a few minutes.

Consume with passion and a bottle of brown ale!

KW

cinnamon **glazed ham** with **sweet** and **sour** cabbage

This dish is especially good for those who enjoy the combination of sweet and sour flavours. Because I use ham hocks, it is also a relatively inexpensive treat.

SERVES 4

2 ham hocks
75 g (3 oz) carrots, roughly chopped
115 g (4 oz) onion, studded with cloves
75 g (3 oz) celery, roughly chopped
50 g (2 oz) fennel bulb, roughly chopped
50 g (2 oz) leeks, roughly chopped
bouquet garni
4 tbsp Dijon mustard
6 tbsp soft brown sugar
2 tsp cinnamon
75 g (3 oz) unsalted butter, chilled and cubed

FOR THE CABBAGE

225 g (8 oz) Savoy cabbage, cleaned and sliced
2 tbsp olive oil
2 cloves garlic, crushed
2 tsp black peppercorns, crushed
75 g (3 oz) white onion, sliced
25 g (1 oz) sultanas
50 g (2 oz) soft brown sugar
50 g (2 oz) balsamic vinegar
50 ml (2 fl oz) dry white wine
pinch of cardamom
salt and freshly ground black pepper

Place the ham hocks in a pan of cold water and allow to soak for 12 hours. Drain and wash the hocks in running cold water. Return to the pan and cover with fresh cold water. Bring slowly to the boil, then drain. Top with cold water and add the vegetables and bouquet garni. Bring slowly to the boil, reduce the heat and simmer for 1–1¼ hours.

Mix together Dijon mustard, soft brown sugar and cinnamon. Transfer the ham hocks from the liquid and remove any skin and excess fat. Place the trimmed hocks on a baking tray and cover with half of the mustard mixture. Place in a preheated oven at 200°C/400°F/Gas 6 for 10 minutes, re-coat with the remaining mustard mixture and cook for a further 15 minutes until golden brown.

Strain the ham stock into a clean pan and bring to the boil. Add the cabbage and cook for 2–3 minutes. Remove from the stock and place to one side, reserving the stock.

Heat the olive oil in a saucepan, add the garlic, black peppercorns and onion, cook gently for 4–5 minutes; add the cabbage, sultanas and soft brown sugar.

In a small pan, heat the balsamic vinegar and dry white wine with the cardamom and reduce by two thirds. Add this to the cabbage and season with salt and freshly ground pepper. Pour 300 ml (½ pint) of ham stock into the pan that contained the balsamic vinegar reduction (taste the stock first to ensure that it's not salty). Bring to the boil and whisk in the chilled unsalted butter. Turn off the heat once the stock thickens.

To serve, place the cabbage on a plate, carve the ham over the cabbage and spoon a little sauce around the dish.

KW

fillet of **pork** with a **sweet chilli** and **mango salsa**

I am a great fan of British pork, especially organic. We filmed a breeder in Yorkshire whose happy pigs produced the loveliest meat I have tasted. Nevertheless, this dish packs flavour into pork by way of a fabulous stuffing with an array of cosmopolitan ingredients – once again reflecting the international influences upon British taste.

SERVES 4

2 x 225 g (8 oz) pork fillets
50 g (2 oz) dried ready-to-eat prunes
75 g (3 oz) dried ready-to-eat apricots
1 large apple, cored
4 tbsp chopped coriander
vegetable oil, for frying
115 g (4 oz) courgettes, grated
115 g (4 oz) carrots, grated
50 g (2 oz) onion, grated
2 small eggs
50 g (2 oz) plain flour
salt and freshly ground black pepper

FOR THE SALSA
2 medium mangoes, finely chopped
1 large red onion, finely chopped
2 cloves garlic, smashed
2.5 cm (1 inch) fresh ginger root, finely chopped
1 tbsp chopped coriander
4 red chillies, halved, deseeded and chopped
juice and zest of 1 lemon
2 tbsp sweet chilli sauce

Cut the pork fillets in half lengthways. Place on a cutting board, cover with clear film and flatten using a rolling pin.

Place the prunes, apricots and apple in a food processor and coarsely blend. Remove from the bowl, add the chopped coriander and season with salt and pepper. Spread the fruit stuffing over the pork fillets and roll them up, like a Swiss roll. Secure with string and season with salt and pepper.

Heat a little vegetable oil in a frying pan, add the pork fillets and lightly cook on all sides until the meat is sealed. Place the fillets in a preheated oven at 220°C/425°F/Gas 5 and cook for 10–14 minutes, until thoroughly cooked.

Mix the grated courgettes, carrots and onion together and season with a little salt and pepper. Beat the eggs and whisk in the flour to form a paste, then mix through the grated vegetables. Divide the mixture into 4 equal portions. Reheat the frying pan in which the pork was sealed, and add the vegetable portions. Gently press them into four rösti shapes. Cook gently, browning on both sides.

Make the salsa; place the mango and red onion in a bowl and add the garlic, ginger, coriander, chillies, lemon juice and zest. Bind all these ingredients with the sweet chilli sauce.

To serve, remove the pork from the oven, discard the string and carve the meat into 4 cm/1½ inch rounds. Put a vegetable rösti in the centre of each large individual dinner plate, place some pork rounds on top and surround with the salsa.

KW

apple fritters with apple honey

My sons Kevin II and Jonathan often have 'I need food now' attacks. You can make this batter in the morning and keep it in the refrigerator, ready to make a few pancakes later in the day. This will buy you time while you prepare a meal.

MAKES 25–30

FOR THE FRITTERS
115 g (4 oz) flour
115 g (4 oz) cornmeal, ground fine
3 tbsp sugar
2 tsp baking powder
1 tsp ground coriander
1 tsp ground nutmeg
½ tsp cinnamon
½ tsp salt
50 ml (2 fl oz) buttermilk
350 ml (12 fl oz) apple cider, filtered
2 large apples, cored and cut into long julienne strips
vegetable oil, for deep frying

FOR THE APPLE HONEY
750 ml (1¼ pints) apple cider, filtered
1 tbsp honey

Make the apple honey. In a saucepan, boil the apple cider until reduced to just less than 175 ml (6 fl oz) and stir in the honey. Bring back to a boil and remove from the heat. This can be made days before; once cooked, cover and refrigerate. Reheat before serving.

In a large bowl, sift together the flour, cornmeal, sugar, baking powder, coriander, nutmeg, cinnamon and salt. Stir in the buttermilk and apple cider. Stir in the apples well and let the batter rest for 10 minutes.

Heat 5–7.5 cm/2–3 inches of oil in a heavy saucepan to 180°C/350°F. Drop the batter, by tablespoons, into the oil and fry 4–5 fritters at a time until golden brown, about 3 minutes. Once cooked, place the fritters on a baking sheet covered with kitchen paper to drain. Make sure the oil heats up to temperature for the next batch. Serve with the apple honey.

KB

pear and raisin clafoutis with mascarpone

This is basically a sweet batter, not unlike a Yorkshire pudding or pancake mixture. The mascarpone is optional and can be changed for anything from ice cream to custard.

SERVES 4

- 4 ripe pears, peeled, cored and sliced
- 50 g (2 oz) soft muscovado sugar
- zest and juice of 1 lemon
- 1 glass brandy
- 225 g (8 oz) plain flour
- 75 g (3 oz) icing sugar
- 50 ml (2 fl oz) milk
- 90 ml (3 fl oz) whipping cream
- 3 eggs, beaten
- 50 g (2 oz) plump raisins
- 2 tbsp runny honey
- 175 g (6 oz) mascarpone cheese
- icing sugar, to decorate

Place the pears in a saucepan and add the muscovado sugar, lemon juice, lemon zest and brandy. Gently cook until the fruit is soft. Remove from the liquid and place on one side. Reduce the cooking liquid by two thirds.

Mix together the flour and icing sugar using an electric mixer; when the mixture is at a creamy stage slowly add the milk and cream. Once this is blended, add the reduced cooking liquid and then gently beat in the eggs until the batter is smooth.

Put the pears in a lightly greased ovenproof dish, sprinkle with raisins and pour the batter over the fruit. Bake in a preheated oven at 190°C/375°F/Gas 5 for 45 minutes.

Mix the honey with the mascarpone and lightly whip.

To serve, dust the clafoutis with icing sugar and serve the honeyed mascarpone on the side.

KW

guava turnovers

My mother in law Aleida Barrera, who lived with me and the boys after the divorce, turned me on to Guava Paste. Little Kevin says it is just like quince jelly, it comes solid and slices from a block to serve with cheese. I like it on toast with sliced cream cheese. Some in-laws are great, I know.

SERVES 6

4 x 1¼ oz ready-made all butter puff pastry squares
115 g (4 oz) guava paste
1 tsp fresh lemon juice
⅛ tsp ground allspice
1 tsp icing sugar

On a lightly floured surface, roll each piece of puff pastry into a 13 cm/5 inch square. Place the squares on a baking sheet. Slice the guava paste 3 mm/⅛ inch thick. Put one-quarter of the paste in the centre of each pastry square, drizzle with ¼ tsp lemon juice and dust with a tiny pinch of allspice. Lightly moisten the edges of the pastry and fold each square into a triangle. Crimp the edges to seal. Cover with clear film and refrigerate until chilled.

Bake the turnovers in a preheated oven at 190°F/375°F/Gas 5 for about 20 minutes or until puffed and golden brown. Place on a rack and let cool for at least 30 minutes. Sift icing sugar over the turnovers and serve.

KB

sopaipillas

This dish was traditionally served between courses of a very spicy meal to calm down the palate. Bite off the corners of your sopaipillas and fill with honey. Yum!

MAKES 24

25 g (1 oz) dried yeast
50 ml (2 fl oz) warm water
300 ml (½ pint) milk, scalded
450 g (1 lb) flour, sifted
1½ tsp salt
1 tsp baking powder
1 tbsp sugar
15 g (½ oz) shortening
vegetable oil, for deep frying
icing sugar, to serve

Dissolve the yeast in the warm water. When the scalded milk cools to room temperature, add the yeast mixture.

Combine the flour, salt, baking powder and sugar and mix well. Cut the shortening into the dry ingredients. Add the milk mixture to this and work into a dough.

Knead the dough 15–20 times and let it rest for 10 minutes. Roll the dough into 5 mm/¼ inch thickness and cut into 5 cm/2 inch size triangles. Deep fry in batches in vegetable oil at 200°C/400°F until golden and puffed up. Drain on kitchen paper and keep warm while frying the remaining triangles.

Sprinkle icing sugar or cinnamon and honey over the top and serve.

KB

blood orange and walnut curd tarts

A tasty treat, these are delicious served warm or cold; in fact, they are so good they never last very long in my household.

SERVES 4

275 g (10 oz) plain flour
2 tsp icing sugar, plus a little more for dusting
pinch of salt
115 g (4 oz) butter
2 egg yolks
4 tbsp water, cold
4 blood oranges
4 eggs, beaten
275 g (10 oz) curd cheese
1 small glass Cointreau
75 g (3 oz) caster sugar
50 g (2 oz) chopped walnuts
lemon ice cream or lemon custard, to serve

Place the flour, icing sugar, salt and butter in a food processor and blend to a fine, sandy texture. Pour in the egg yolks and water, mix to form a smooth dough. Remove the dough from the machine and gently knead.

Divide the dough into four and roll out to line four non-stick 10 cm/4 inch pastry tins. Use a fork to prick the base of the pastry, cover with greaseproof paper, fill with baking beans and cook in a preheated oven 200°C/400°F/Gas 6 for 6 minutes. Remove the pastry tins from the oven.

For the filling, grate the zest of 4 blood oranges and then squeeze the juice from 3 of the oranges into a bowl, add the beaten eggs and slowly blend in the curd cheese, Cointreau and sugar to form a wet batter.

Pour the batter into the pastry cases and sprinkle the walnuts on top.

Cook in the oven for 10–12 minutes, until just set. When the tarts have cooled a little, remove from the tins and dust with icing sugar. Serve with lemon ice cream or lemon custard.

KW

chocolate flan

This unusual combination is a real treat. You could add some rum or brandy to the milk for a bit of zing.

SERVES 12

350 g (12 oz) sugar
2 tbsp fresh lemon juice
1 litre (1¾ pints) milk
175 g (6 oz) plain chocolate, chopped
8 large eggs
½ tsp vanilla essence
¼ tsp cinnamon

In a saucepan, combine 200 g (7 oz) of the sugar with the lemon juice. Using a wooden spoon, stir over medium heat until the sugar dissolves, then cook, stirring occasionally, until the sugar turns deep brown. Pour the hot caramel into a 1.75 litre (3 pint) metal ring mould. Tilt the mould to coat the sides with the caramel using a spoon as needed.

In a heavy saucepan, combine the milk with the remaining sugar stirring occasionally until sugar is dissolved. Add the chocolate, cover and remove from the heat. Set aside until the chocolate is melted. Stir.

In a bowl, lightly beat the eggs. Slowly whisk in the hot milk, vanilla, and cinnamon until thoroughly combined. Strain the custard into a large measuring jug, then pour it into the ring mould. Cover the flan loosely with foil and place the mould in a baking dish.

Pour in enough hot water to reach halfway up the side of the mould. Bake in a preheated oven at 150°C/300°F/Gas 2 for about 1 hour 15 minutes or until flan is set but still shakes in the middle.

Remove the mould from the baking dish. Let the flan cool to room temperature, then refrigerate overnight.

Run a knife around the sides of the mould, cover with a large plate and invert. Cut the flan into wedges and serve.

KB

steamed **orange pudding** with a bay leaf custard

It is possible to cook this pudding in a microwave using exactly the same ingredients and method – but consult your manual for cooking times.

SERVES 6

FOR THE PUDDING
175 g (6 oz) self-raising flour
finely grated zest of 6 oranges and juice of 2 oranges
175 g (6 oz) suet
175 g (6 oz) caster sugar
175 g (6 oz) white breadcrumbs
1 small glass Grand Marnier or Cointreau
2 medium eggs, lightly beaten
orange zest, to decorate

FOR THE BAY LEAF CUSTARD
8 egg yolks
75 g (3 oz) caster sugar
300 ml (½ pint) milk
300 ml (½ pint) whipping cream
4 bay leaves
1 vanilla pod

For the pudding, place the flour, finely grated orange zest, suet, caster sugar and breadcrumbs in a large bowl and mix together. Pour in the orange juice, liqueur and eggs and beat to form a batter. Place the mixture into six greased and floured 150 ml (¼ pint) pudding dishes, until the dishes are three-quarters full. Cover loosely with buttered greaseproof paper and steam in a large saucepan of simmering water for 45–50 minutes. The water should come up to no more than one-third of the sides of the dishes.

For the bay leaf custard, in a bowl, beat together the egg yolks and sugar until the mixture is light and fluffy. Pour the milk and cream into a pan, add the bay leaves, split the vanilla pod to release the seeds and add to the pan; bring to the boil and pour the hot liquid onto the egg yolk and sugar mixture, whisking together. Place the bowl over a pan of hot water and stir until the sauce thickens. Remove from the heat and strain into a jug.

Place a small pudding in the centre of a large soup bowl, flood the bowl with custard and place some orange zest in the centre of the pudding. Serve immediately.

KW

yorkshire **gingerbread** with stilton

This keeps well if stored in an airtight container and after a little while it will become even more rich and moist. It is also delicious when served plain with a cup of strong Indian tea.

SERVES 6

130 g (4½ oz) butter, softened
130 g (4½ oz) dark muscovado sugar, sieved
200 g (7 oz) golden syrup
225 g (8 oz) plain flour, sifted
4 tsp ground ginger
1 tsp baking soda
150 ml (¼ pint) milk
1 egg
225 g (8 oz) crystallized ginger, diced
zest of 1 lemon
Stilton cheese and pickles, to serve

Using an electric whisk, beat together the butter, sugar, syrup, flour, ginger, baking soda, milk and egg for about 5 minutes, until the mixture is pale and thick.

Add the crystallized ginger and lemon zest and mix through.

Transfer the mixture to a greased and lined 20 cm/8 inch square cake tin and bake in a preheated oven at 160°C/325°F/Gas 3 for 1 hour 10 minutes. The cake should be firm but moist when cooked. Allow to cool and remove from the baking tin.

Serve cold with wedges of Stilton cheese and pickles.

KW

chilli **lemonade**

Chilli doesn't just add heat to dishes, it also adds flavour. This unusual combination of citrus and spice is a real thirst quencher. Here the chilli doesn't overpower the drink, but gives it the kind of bite you normally associate with a good ginger beer. It's also a doddle to make.

handful of dried red chillies
1 litre (1¾ pints) water
juice of 3 lemons
juice of 3 limes
sugar to taste

Soak the dried chillies in about 250 ml (8 fl oz) of the water for 10 minutes.

Add the lemon and lime juice to a large jug and add sugar to taste; add the remaining water, stirring to dissolve sugar.

Strain the chilli soaking water and add to the jug.

Serve with ice cubes.

KB

WALES

Trying some elk in Big Kevin's kitchen.

The theme here is mountain cookery. Montana is home to the Rockies, the range of mountains that winds its way through the state and northwards into Canada. The black mountains of Wales are mere dumplings in comparison, far more cultivated and far less wild.

In Montana it's legal to carry a firearm everywhere except banks and places selling alcohol. We discovered that the Wild West is alive and well in Tixie's bar at Ovando, just 40 miles east of Missoula (check your guns at the door). From here we ventured into the Bob Marshall Wilderness on the Monture trail in search of wild elk. Elk is also farmed in these parts, but the taste of wild elk has no comparison, although some say it has an equal in wild buffalo. The only way to get it is to shoot it, since it is strictly controlled by the Federal Food

AND MONTANA

and Drug Administration, to the point that virtually no one sells it. So step one in our elk recipe was to catch our elk, which involves a day's ride into the wilderness armed with a guide, a permit and a .44. If you don't happen to have a supply of wild elk on your doorstep, you can substitute venison or beef in all the elk recipes in this chapter.

We also wanted huckleberries for the recipe, but they had been in short supply this year, so much so that the bears who tuck into the berries before their winter hibernation had been forced out of the hills and into folks' trash cans. We settled for cranberries.

In Wales we ventured into the Black Mountains, more a walk in the country than an adventure. Like much of Britain, Wales has a lot of rabbits. The history of rabbit damage in Europe goes back a long way. In about 50BC, the inhabitants of the islands of Majorca and Minorca sent a deputation to the Romans soliciting that new lands might be given to them as they were quite driven out of their country by rabbits. The terrible viral disease of myxomatosis was introduced to the rabbit population in the 1950s to control numbers. However the rabbits have mostly bred their way out of this, so now plagues of them are reported from time to time across the country. Rabbit is a very good food that has lost its popularity, presumably due to the fact that they are also family pets. At one time in Wales it was a commodity for rural families, many of whom survived entirely on the sale of rabbits in the markets. It is one of the few wild meats available in the UK and as such should be celebrated.

Dolly and Buddy carried the Kevins into the Bob Marshal Wilderness near Ovando, Montana.

Tom Ide, our expert and patient guide on the Monture trail.

leek and watercress soup with herbed croûtons

I love this soup nearly as much as I love my car! It is the sort of dish that pleads to be eaten when you are feeling tired and jaded. It has great colour, a fabulous texture and is so healthy.

SERVES 6

175 g (6 oz) butter
675 g (1½ lb) floury potatoes, peeled and sliced
3 cloves garlic, crushed
175 g (6 oz) leeks, sliced
1.75 litres (3 pints) chicken or vegetable stock
400 g (14 oz) watercress
50 ml (2 fl oz) olive oil
2 slices bread, crusts removed and cubed
1 tbsp dried mixed herbs
salt and freshly ground black pepper
6 tbsp whipping cream (optional), to serve

Melt the butter, add the potatoes, garlic and leeks, and cook without colouring for 5 minutes. Add the stock and bring to the boil. Cover and allow to cook gently for 25–30 minutes until the vegetables are soft.

Add the watercress and cook for a further 5 minutes, allow to cool a little and then liquidize in a blender, in batches if necessary. Season with salt and pepper.

For the croûtons, heat the oil in a frying pan, add the pieces of bread and sprinkle the dried herbs onto the croûtons. Turn until the croûtons become golden brown.

Serve in a bowl, top with a little cream or yogurt and add the croûtons.

KW

forest mushroom frittata

What a lovely way to serve fresh English mushrooms! All of the flavour gathered in lightly cooked egg with a hint of superb British cheese. The wider the variety of mushrooms you use, the more intense the flavour will be.

SERVES 4

50 g (2 oz) butter
2 tbsp olive oil
50 g (2 oz) shallots, finely diced
2 cloves garlic, smashed
1 tsp crushed black peppercorns
1 tsp paprika
2 tbsp chopped fresh coriander
150 g (5 oz) forest mushrooms, sliced
6 eggs
25 g (1 oz) any British hard cheese, grated
25 g (1 oz) white breadcrumbs
salt
tomato and basil salad, to serve

Heat the butter and olive oil in a frying pan; add the shallots, garlic, peppercorns, paprika, coriander and mushrooms. Cook for 10 minutes.

Mix the eggs, grated cheese and breadcrumbs, season with salt and beat lightly. Add the mushroom mixture to the beaten eggs and mix through.

Pour the mixture into a lightly greased ovenproof dish and cook in a preheated oven at 190°C/375°F/Gas 5 for 18–20 minutes until set. Finish by colouring the top of the frittata under a hot grill until golden brown.

Serve with a lightly dressed tomato and basil salad.

KW

laver-bread noodles with a bacon and cockle sauce

I adore this recipe because it uses traditional Welsh ingredients to create an exciting European dish.

SERVES 6

450 g (1 lb) plain flour (Italian '0-0' flour is best)
½ tsp salt
4 medium eggs
1 tsp olive oil
50 g (2 oz) laver-bread, excess moisture squeezed out

FOR THE SAUCE
1 tbsp olive oil
50 g (2 oz) shallots, peeled and finely diced
2 cloves garlic, peeled and crushed
50 g (2 oz) streaky bacon, rind removed and finely diced
1 tbsp fennel leaves, chopped
120 ml (4 fl oz) dry white wine
250 ml (8 fl oz) whipping cream
50 g (2 oz) shelled cockles
salt and freshly ground black pepper

Sift the flour and salt together onto a clean pastry board. Make a well in the centre and add the eggs and oil. Gradually incorporate the flour to form a smooth dough. If the dough feels dry, work it a little harder. The alternative and, in my opinion, the best way to make this is to place all the ingredients in a food processor, switch it on, stand back and watch it happen!

Now add the laver bread. Be sure that you have removed as much moisture as possible. Knead the dough for 5 minutes, cover with clear film and refrigerate for at least 30 minutes.

Once again technology has a role to play here – buy a pasta machine that will enable you to roll the dough perfectly. Alternatively, divide the dough into four, roll out each piece as thinly as possible and cut into ribbons.

The pasta can either be cooked straight away or, if you prefer, placed in an airtight container and refrigerated to use the following day. To cook, place the pasta in boiling salted water for 1–2 minutes and drain.

To make the sauce, heat the olive oil in a saucepan and add the shallots, garlic and bacon. Cook for 3–4 minutes and then add the fennel leaves, followed by the white wine. Boil the liquid until it has reduced by a half, and add the cream. Drop in the cockles and reduce by a further one-third. Season with salt and pepper.

To serve, mix the sauce with the noodles.

KW

warm salad of **rabbit sausage** with redcurrant compote

If you cannot or do not want to use pig's caul, then use rindless streaky bacon. For best results stretch the bacon to make it as thin as possible by simply pressing with the side of a kitchen knife.

SERVES 4–6

450 g (1 lb) rabbit meat, including liver, coarsely minced or chopped
2 shallots, finely diced
2 cloves garlic, chopped
1 small egg, beaten
2 tbsp yogurt or soured cream
2 tsp mixed herbs
4 tbsp chopped fresh coriander
½ tsp ground cardamom
pinch of cayenne
2 tbsp brandy
40 g (1 ½ oz) breadcrumbs
3 tbsp olive oil, plus extra for roasting
50 g (2 oz) pig's caul
8 plum tomatoes, quartered
2 red peppers, deseeded and cut into eighths
2 green peppers, deseeded and cut into eighths
vegetable oil, for frying
coarse sea salt and freshly ground black pepper

FOR THE REDCURRANT COMPOTE
40 g (1½ oz) sugar
2 tbsp cider vinegar
sprig of rosemary
2 tbsp orange juice
275 g (10 oz) redcurrants, washed and picked over

Place the meat in a bowl and add the shallots, garlic, egg, yogurt or cream, mixed herbs, 1 tbsp of the coriander, the cardamom, cayenne, brandy, breadcrumbs and a little salt and pepper. Knead the mixture together and mould into little sausage shapes each weighing about 50 g (2 oz).

Mix the remaining coriander with the olive oil and brush over each sausage; cover by wrapping the whole sausage in a piece of caul. Chill in the refrigerator for 1 hour.

Meanwhile, make the redcurrant compote; place the sugar, vinegar, rosemary and orange juice in a small saucepan. Heat gently until the sugar dissolves. Increase the heat and cook until it forms a light syrup. Stir in the redcurrants and cook until they begin to burst. Remove the syrup from the heat and leave to cool, it will thicken as it cools.

Place the tomatoes and peppers in a roasting tin and season with salt and pepper. Drizzle a little olive oil over and cook in a preheated oven at 200°F/400°F/Gas 6 for 40 minutes.

Cook the sausage in a frying pan with a little hot oil until browned and cooked through. Place the roasted vegetables in the centre of the plate, place a sausage on top and spoon a little of the compote on one side.

KW

welsh rarebit with a poached egg

This is a great little starter or snack – not to be confused with Shirley Bassey although she's one of my favourites (and big Kev has a thing about older women especially those from Wales)!

SERVES 3

15 g (½ oz) butter
15 g (½ oz) flour
6 tbsp milk
2 tbsp Worcestershire sauce
pinch of cayenne pepper
1 tsp prepared English mustard
5 eggs
50 g (2 oz) strong Cheddar cheese, grated
6 slices bread
butter, for spreading
salt and freshly ground black pepper

Melt the butter in a pan, add the flour and cook gently for 2 minutes. Gradually add the milk, a little at a time and stir to form a smooth sauce. Remove from the heat. Add the Worcestershire sauce, cayenne pepper, mustard and a little salt and pepper. Separate 2 of the eggs and whisk the yolks into the sauce and then beat in the grated cheese.

Whisk the 2 egg whites until they are stiff and use a metal spoon to fold them into the cheese mixture.

Poach the remaining 3 eggs in a pan of simmering water containing a little salt and just a touch of vinegar. Remove from the water and drain on kitchen paper.

Toast the bread and butter on one side. Spread a thin layer of the cheese mixture over the toast and place a poached egg on top. Pour the remainder of the cheese mixture over the egg and place under a hot grill until golden brown.

KW

tim's **elk jerky**

When you get deep into the wilderness, you never know when you're next going to eat. So every good cowboy carries his strip of jerky, and every great cowboy makes his own jerky. When we arrived, Tom's son Tim had just made a fresh batch from an elk he had shot a couple of weeks before. Of course if you ain't got wild elk (and you wouldn't unless you've been to Montana recently) you could try salmon, beef, venison or even lamb. But don't try wild boar, pork or bear: since the meat is not cooked, there's a risk of trichinosis.

250 ml (8 fl oz) ready-made teriyaki sauce
120 ml (4 fl oz) soy sauce
2 cloves garlic, crushed
250 ml (8 fl oz) red wine
900 g–1.5 kg (2–3 lb) elk, thinly sliced

In a bowl, combine the teriyaki sauce, soy sauce, garlic and wine. Add the thinly sliced elk; cover and marinate in the refrigerator for 12 hours.

Place the elk strips in a smoker and smoke away from the heat for 20–24 hours. If you do not have a smoker, this can be done in a low oven for 6 hours.

KB

whipped mashed **potato** with **goat's cheese** and **bacon**

This dish will enhance any main course, especially lamb and fish but I like it as a snack or starter in its own right, especially since the UK now produces some of the finest goat's cheese imaginable. It is worth seeking out a smaller producer.

SERVES 4

450 g (1 lb) potatoes
25 g (1 oz) butter
75 g (3 oz) lean bacon, finely diced
1 clove garlic, crushed
2 tbsp snipped chives
2 tbsp extra-virgin olive oil
175 g (6 oz) goat's cheese, softest available
salt and freshly ground black pepper

Cook the potatoes in boiling salted water, drain and return to the pan on a low heat. Mash to a purée.

Heat the butter in a frying pan, add the bacon, garlic and chives and cook until the bacon is crisp.

Add the olive oil and goat's cheese to the puréed potatoes and, using a wooden spoon, beat until light and fluffy; season with salt and pepper, mix in the bacon mixture and serve.

KW

glamorgan sausage
with a caper and garlic dressing

This meat-free sausage is absolutely delightful served as a starter with a crisp well dressed selection of leaves. You could also make dinky little ones and serve them for snacks or with cocktails.

SERVES 4

FOR THE SAUSAGE
675 g (1½ lb) canned cannellini beans
2 cloves garlic, chopped
115 g (4 oz) shallots, finely chopped
2 tbsp flat leaf parsley, chopped
115 g (4 oz) Glamorgan, Lancashire or Cheshire cheese, grated
3 eggs
75 g (3 oz) plain flour
75 g (3 oz) fine breadcrumbs
vegetable oil, for deep frying
salt and freshly ground black pepper

FOR THE DRESSING
300 ml (½ pint) mayonnaise
50 g (2 oz) capers, chopped
1 clove garlic, chopped and crushed
1 tbsp parsley, chopped

Drain the beans and place in a food blender; process until they are a purée. Transfer the bean purée to a bowl and add the garlic, shallots, parsley and grated cheese. Beat 1 egg and add to the purée; mix together and season with salt and freshly ground black pepper.

Divide the mixture into your preferred portion size and mould into a sausage shape. Beat the remaining eggs in a shallow dish. Dip the bean sausages in flour, then beaten egg and finally breadcrumbs. Chill for 15 minutes in the refrigerator.

Meanwhile, make the dressing. Put the mayonnaise in a serving dish and mix in the capers, garlic and chopped parsley.

Deep fry the sausages in hot oil until golden brown and serve with the garlic dressing.

KW

chicken and bacon pithiviers with a wild mushroom sauce

A rich recipe for those occasions when you want a special treat.

SERVES 4

175 ml (6 fl oz) whipping cream
2 breasts chicken, skinned
50 g (2 oz) back bacon, diced
75 g (3 oz) chicken thighs, skinned, boned and minced
½ tbsp black peppercorns, finely crushed
pinch of grated nutmeg
pinch of ground cloves
1 tbsp chopped fresh tarragon
50 g (2 oz) spring onion, white part only, finely chopped
450 g (1 lb) puff pastry
2 eggs, beaten
salt and freshly ground black pepper

FOR THE SAUCE

50 g (2 oz) butter
50 g (2 oz) shallots, finely grated
2 cloves garlic, smashed
50 g (2 oz) mixed wild mushrooms
1 small glass white wine
1 tbsp Dijon mustard
250 ml (8 fl oz) whipping cream
salt and freshly ground black pepper

Place the 175 ml (6 fl oz) cream in a small pan and bring to the boil; simmer until it is reduced by half, and cool.

Remove the fillets from underneath the chicken breasts, roughly chop and place in a bowl. Cut the breasts in half and then make an incision across each half, to create an opening.

To the roughly chopped chicken fillets, add the diced bacon, minced thighs, crushed peppercorns, grated nutmeg, ground cloves, tarragon, spring onions; mix together. Mix in the reduced cream and season with salt. Fill each chicken breast with the mixture and refrigerate.

Roll out the puff pastry to 3 mm/⅛ inch thick and cut four 12 cm/4½ inch circles and four 15 cm/6 inch circles. Place a chicken portion on each small circle and brush the pastry edge with beaten egg. Place a larger circle on top, sealing the edges. Brush well with beaten egg and refrigerate for 20 minutes.

Using the point of a knife, make a small incision through the centre of the pastry and then lightly draw the knife neatly down the pastry from the centre to the edge. Repeat this procedure around the pie to create a pattern; but do not penetrate right through the pastry. Brush with beaten egg and bake in a preheated oven at 200°C/400°F/ Gas 6 for 30 minutes until golden brown and the chicken is cooked through.

To make the sauce, heat the butter in a saucepan, add the chopped shallots and garlic and cook gently for 2–3 minutes. Add the mushrooms and cook for a further 3–4 minutes. Add the white wine and cook until the sauce is reduced by half, then add the mustard and cream. Bring to the boil and simmer until the sauce reduces by one-third. Season with the salt and black pepper. Serve with the pithiviers.

KW

grilled **pork tenderloins** with apples and onions

This is another one from Valerie's camp fire. Picking your pork carefully is the key to this dish. She uses only local pork, hand-reared by someone she knows looks after the piggies and is of course organic. Like that of many of the earlier settlers here, its origin is German, especially with the onions and apples with caraway seeds.

SERVES 4

3 garlic cloves, crushed
2 tbsp lime juice
2 tbsp olive oil
2 tbsp thyme leaves
1 shallot, minced
1 tbsp very finely chopped fresh ginger root
900 g (2 lb) pork tenderloins
½ tsp each salt and freshly ground black pepper

FOR THE APPLES AND ONION
2 apples, cored and sliced
50 g (2 oz) butter, cut into pieces
50 g (2 oz) brown sugar
2 tbsp cider vinegar
½ tsp caraway seeds
2 large onions, peeled and sliced
freshly ground black pepper

In a shallow dish, mix the garlic, lime juice, olive oil, thyme, shallot, ginger, salt and pepper. Add the pork, turning well to coat with the spices. Let the pork sit in the spices for 30 minutes.

Meanwhile, make the apples and onion. In a heavy frying pan, place a layer of apples and sprinkle half of the butter, brown sugar and cider vinegar and all the caraway over the apples. Add the sliced onion in a layer, and then the remaining butter, brown sugar and cider vinegar. Season with ground black pepper.

Place the pan under a hot grill or over high heat on the hob. Cook for 15–20 minutes until the apples and onions have softened and caramelized with light brown edges. The apples and onions will keep warm in the skillet off the heat until ready to serve.

Grill the pork on a stove-top grill pan over a medium to high heat or under a hot grill for about 15 minutes each side. This should produce a nice medium-well doneness. Place the pork on a platter, cover with foil and let rest for 5 minutes. Slice and serve with the apples and onion.

KB

roast **sea bass** with **elephant garlic** and laver sauce

This is a perfect example of the way in which the subtle flavours of fish can be enhanced by the use of good quality ingredients, to produce a dish that is full of flavour and yet still light in essence.

SERVES 4

4 portions of sea bass, filleted with skin left on
2 tbsp olive oil
1 tbsp chopped dill
juice of ½ lemon
24 cloves elephant garlic, not peeled
24 shallots, not peeled
50 g (2 oz) butter
50 g (2 oz) lean bacon, finely diced
120 ml (4 fl oz) dry white wine
175 g (6 oz) laver purée
1 tsp lemon juice
salt and freshly ground black pepper
bunch of chives, trimmed to 10 cm/4 in

With a sharp knife make 4 incisions across the skin of the fish. Mix together the olive oil, chopped dill and juice of ½ lemon. Brush this over the skinned side of the sea bass. Season with a little salt and pepper and place skin side down in a preheated, lightly oiled griddle pan. Place in a hot oven for 2 minutes. Carefully turn the fish, surround with the garlic and shallots and drizzle a little of the oil mixture over them. Return the pan to the oven and cook for a further 8–10 minutes until the fish is cooked.

Meanwhile prepare the sauce. Heat the butter in a saucepan, add the bacon and cook gently for 3–4 minutes. Pour on the wine and reduce by half, add the laver purée and 1 tsp of lemon juice and gently heat. Season with salt and freshly ground black pepper.

Remove the fish from the oven. Carefully pour the juices from the griddle pan into the laver sauce and mix through.

To serve, place the sea bass fillets, skin side up, on the centre of each plate. Spoon a little of the sauce around the fish and place three evenly divided groups of shallots and garlic around the plate; top with the trimmed chives.

KW

spatchcocked citrus and soy poussin

This is my favourite summer dish, great for impromptu summer dining in the garden on a sunny evening with a glass of chilled white wine.

SERVES 4

4 poussin
2 tbsp olive oil
fresh coriander, to garnish

FOR THE MARINADE
zest strips and juice of 1 orange
zest strips and juice of 1 lemon
zest strips and juice of 1 lime
3 tbsp soy sauce
2 tbsp olive oil
1 tbsp honey
2 garlic cloves, chopped
1 tbsp chopped fresh ginger root
2 red chillies, deseeded and roughly chopped
salt and freshly ground black pepper

In a large bowl, combine all the marinade ingredients and whisk to emulsify.

To prepare the poussin, place each bird on a chopping board, cut off the feet above the joint, the wing tips and middle section of the wings. Place each bird breast side down and with a sharp knife cut along each side of the backbone from the tail to the neck. Remove the bone and reserve for making stock.

Clean the inside of the bird by wiping with kitchen paper. Trim the skin and open the bird out, snip the wishbone in half or remove it. Set the bird breast side up and press sharply down with the heel of the hand on the breastbone to flatten the bird completely. With a sharp knife, make a small slit through the skin between the breast and thigh on both sides and tuck each leg down through the slits.

Place the birds in a ceramic dish, pour the marinade over and refrigerate for 2–4 hours.

Heat the oil in a large frying pan and place a spatchcocked poussin, skin side down, in the pan. Fry over a moderately high heat about 8 minutes on each side until a nice golden colour. Lower the heat and finish cooking; it is crucial that the bird is cooked right through. Keep warm while cooking the remaining birds.

You can also barbecue the birds, but my preferred method is in the oven where the temperature and cooking times are more controllable.

KW

game pie

Game pie is a great British tradition and is marvellous with home-made chutney.

SERVES 8

FOR THE MARINADE
150 ml (¼ pint) white wine
6 juniper berries
2 cloves garlic, crushed
1 bouquet garni
2 bay leaves
16 black peppercorns, crushed

FOR THE FILLING
450 g (1 lb) venison, trimmed off the bone
225 g (8 oz) rabbit meat, trimmed off the bone
225 g (8 oz) pheasant, trimmed off the bone
450 g (1 lb) sausage meat
175 g (6 oz) streaky bacon, diced
1 tsp herbes de Provence
150 ml (¼ pint) red wine
150 ml (¼ pint) chicken or game stock
2 tsp powdered gelatine
salt and freshly ground black pepper

FOR THE PASTRY
450 g (1 lb) plain flour
½ tsp salt
115 g (4 oz) lard
300 ml (½ pint) water
1 egg, beaten, for glazing

Mix together all the ingredients for the marinade in a large dish. Cut the game into long strips and place into the marinade, cover and chill for 24 hours.

Take the game out of the marinade and dry with kitchen paper. Mix together the game, sausage meat, bacon, herbes de Provence and season with salt and ground black pepper.

Make the pastry by sieving the flour and salt together in a large bowl. Heat the lard in the water until it has melted and gradually stir into the flour, mixing to form a smooth dough. Cover the dough with clear film and leave to stand at room temperature for 20 minutes.

Cut two-thirds of the pastry and roll out to line a 20 cm/ 8 inch springform tin with high sides, ensuring that the pastry overlaps the sides of the tin. Put the game mixture into the pastry case and press down so that it fills the case evenly. Brush a little water over the edges of the pastry and roll out the remaining pastry to cover the pie. Seal the pie by nipping the edges together. Cut a small opening in the centre of the pie, wide enough to enable the stock to be poured in later.

Brush the pie generously with the beaten egg and bake in a preheated oven at 200°C/400°F/Gas 6 for 1 hour and then reduce the temperature to 180°C/350°F/Gas 4 and cook for a further hour. If the pastry starts to go too brown, cover with a little baking foil.

In a saucepan, mix together the wine and stock, bring to the boil and add the gelatine. Remove from the heat, whisking to dissolve the gelatine and allow to cool until nearly set.

Remove the pie from the oven and allow to cool slightly. Pour the wine mixture into the pie through the hole in the top. Refrigerate and serve the following day.

KW

braised pigeons in tomato and black olive sauce

Some people are a little squeamish about eating pigeon in the UK, but they are delicious birds when cooked slowly in a rich sauce.

SERVES 4

- 450 g (16 oz) canned tomatoes
- 90 ml (3 fl oz) olive oil
- 4 pigeons, cleaned
- 115 g (4 oz) lean bacon, finely chopped
- 16 button onions, peeled
- 4 cloves garlic, crushed
- 2 tbsp tomato purée
- 1 glass white wine
- 1 bouquet garni
- 50 ml (2 fl oz) balsamic vinegar
- pinch of sugar
- 50 g (2 oz) pitted black olives
- ½ tsp Tabasco sauce
- 3 tbsp chopped fresh coriander
- salt and freshly ground black pepper

Drain the tomatoes, retaining the liquid. Chop the tomatoes and place the liquid in a small saucepan, heat to reduce by half.

Heat the olive oil in a heavy ovenproof casserole. Season the breasts and legs of the pigeons with salt and freshly ground black pepper. Place breast side down in the hot oil and seal on all sides. Remove the pigeons from the pan and place to one side.

Add the chopped bacon to the pan and cook for 2 minutes, then add the button onions, crushed garlic and cook for a further minute. Add the chopped tomatoes, tomato purée and white wine. Allow the liquid to come to the boil and place the pigeons in the sauce, breast side down. Add the bouquet garni, cover with a tight fitting lid and cook in a preheated oven at 220°C/425°F/Gas 7 for 1¾–2 hours.

Reduce the balsamic vinegar by two-thirds by heating it in a small pan with the sugar. Remove the pigeons from the sauce and place on a serving dish. Add the reduced balsamic vinegar to the tomato sauce, season with salt and pepper and discard the bouquet garni. Add the olives, Tabasco sauce and chopped coriander and pour over the birds on the serving dish.

KW

valerie's **elk chilli**

It was great talking to Valerie who is a true foodie. Her cooking skills were fantastic. Imagine cooking for a group of hungry hunters not knowing when they are going to arrive at camp, the nearest store over 100 miles away and only a simple log stove and camp fire to cook on. This dish keeps well and can be heated up at the last minute. You can use venison steaks instead of elk.

SERVES 8

2 tbsp olive oil
450 g (1 lb) elk steak, trimmed and cut into cubes
1 large onion, sliced
3 cloves garlic, diced
500 g (1¼ lb) black beans, soaked overnight
1 bay leaf
2 litres (3½ pints) beef stock
1 green pepper, diced
2 medium cans stewed tomatoes, with juice
1 medium can tomato purée
4 tbsp brown sugar
6 tbsp chilli powder
2 tbsp ground cumin
250 ml (8 fl oz) red wine
salt and red pepper to taste
cream or shredded cheese, to serve

In a heavy casserole, heat the oil over a medium heat. Sauté the elk until just browned. Add the onion and garlic and sauté for another 2–3 minutes. Add the black beans, bay leaf, and 1.5 litres (2 ½ pints) of the beef stock. Bring to the boil, reduce the heat and simmer, covered, for 1 hour 30 minutes.

Add the green pepper, stewed tomatoes, remaining beef stock, tomato sauce, brown sugar, chilli powder and cumin. Simmer for another 30–40 minutes until the beans are tender.

Add the red wine and season with salt and red pepper to taste. You may need to add a little water if the chilli is too thick but remember water dilutes the flavour so do not add too much. Serve with some cream or shredded cheese.

KB

coffee and **sage-roasted elk**

This is camp fire cooking at its best – there's no point going hungry just because you're in the wilderness, but also there's no point in carting too many ingredients to your remote camp site. This recipe uses what's to hand, especially if you're lucky enough to have bagged an elk, and if you haven't then substitute venison, or even good lean beef.

SERVES 6

1.5–1.75 kg (3–4 lb) elk, a roasting joint
1 piece fresh ginger root, sliced
8 cloves garlic, sliced
50 ml (2 fl oz) red wine
475 ml (16 fl oz) coffee
3 tbsp vinegar
2 tbsp Bourbon whiskey
5 rashers streaky bacon
½ tsp sage
⅓ tsp thyme
1 bay leaf
salt and freshly ground black pepper
mashed potatoes, to serve

FOR THE BLACKBERRY SAUCE
225 g (8 oz) blackberries, huckleberries or cranberries
50 g (2 oz) caster sugar (add another 25 g/1 oz if using cranberries)
2 tbsp vinegar
½ tsp dried chilli flakes
zest and juice of 1 orange
½ tsp grated cinnamon stick
2 tbsp Bourbon whiskey
50 g (2 oz) butter, well chilled and diced

Cut slits into the roast and insert slices of ginger and garlic. Place the roast in a large container. Mix together the wine, coffee, vinegar and whiskey; pour over the roast and seal the container with a lid or clear film. Marinate in the refrigerator overnight, turning several times.

In a heavy casserole or roasting tin, cook 1 rasher of bacon until brown. Remove the roast from the container, reserving the marinade. Brown the roast in the casserole, turning to seal both sides.

Place the remaining bacon over the roast in the tin. Sprinkle with salt and pepper. Add the sage, thyme and bay leaf, and pour the marinade over the roast.

Cover the meat and roast it in a preheated oven at 180°C/350°F/Gas 4 for 1½ –2 hours until tender. Remove the meat to a cutting board, reserving the drippings.

Make the blackberry sauce. Put the berries and sugar in a saucepan and cook over a low heat, stirring with a wooden spoon until the berries have collapsed in a purée. Turn the heat to low and add the vinegar, stir and then pour in the pan drippings from the roast. Add the dried chilli flakes, orange zest, orange juice and cinnamon; bring to the boil then simmer gently for 25 minutes, skimming the surface whenever necessary. Add the whiskey and cook for a further 5 minutes. Take pan off the heat and whisk in the butter, a little at a time; season the sauce with salt and pepper.

Slice the roast and serve with mashed potatoes and the blackberry sauce.

KB

country **elk steak** with big sky **buttermilk biscuits**

If you have no elk then venison will do, but make sure it has been well hung. The Highland beef we tried in Mull would be perfect for this dish, as it is not fatty, just like wild elk. The buttermilk 'biscuits' are similar to a British scone in texture.

SERVES 4

4 elk steaks
115 g (4 oz) seasoned flour
vegetable oil, for frying
1 onion, diced
2 tbsp flour
475 ml (16 fl oz) stock
1 tsp each salt, ground black pepper, cayenne pepper

FOR THE BUTTERMILK BISCUITS
275 g (10 oz) plain flour
3 tsp baking powder
1 tsp salt
½ tsp baking soda
75 g (3 oz) butter, melted
250 ml (8 fl oz) buttermilk

Coat the elk steaks in seasoned flour, patting off any excess. In a frying pan, heat some oil and fry the steak until medium rare. In a casserole, heat a little oil and sauté the onion; cover.

Remove the meat from the frying pan and pour off all but a small amount of oil. Brown the 2 tbsp flour in the oil, stirring constantly. Add some of the stock, stirring to mix with the flour and pour into the pan with the onions. Add more stock to make a gravy, then add the meat. Cover and simmer on a low heat for 50–60 minutes, until the meat is tender. Add more stock if necessary as the gravy reduces.

Meanwhile, make the buttermilk biscuits. In a bowl, mix the flour, baking powder, salt and baking soda. Add the butter and buttermilk, mixing to make a sticky dough. On a lightly floured surface, knead the dough and roll into a smooth ball. Roll the dough to 1 cm/½ inch thickness, and cut into rounds. Place dough rounds on a buttered baking sheet. Bake in a preheated oven at 230°C/450°F/Gas 8 for 10–12 minutes.

Serve the casserole with the buttermilk biscuits.

KB

almond **ginger** biscuits

These are great for children's parties, because they can easily be cut into different novelty shapes.

MAKES 48

75 g (3 oz) whole toasted almonds
75 g (3 oz) sugar
115 g (4 oz) flour
2 tsp ground ginger
pinch of salt
115 g (4 oz) unsalted butter, softened
1 tsp vanilla essence

In a food processor, combine the almonds and half of the sugar to create a coarse powder. Place the mixture in a bowl and stir in the flour, ginger and salt.

In a large bowl, beat the butter, remaining sugar and vanilla until well blended. Add the flour mixture and beat until combined. Divide the dough in half and shape into logs. Wrap each log in clear film and chill until firm, at least 3 hours.

Line a baking sheet with parchment paper. Slice the dough logs into 5 mm/¼ inch thick rounds and place 2.5cm/1 inch apart on the baking sheet. Bake in a preheated oven at 180°C/350°F/Gas 4 for 18 minutes or until the edges and bottom are golden. Slide the parchment paper onto cooling racks and let the biscuits cool completely before serving.

KB

cinnamon sugar biscuits

The rimmed edges give a treat with every bite. They tickle your tongue's funny bone!

MAKES 60

150 g (5 oz) flour
¼ tsp baking soda
pinch of salt
115 (4 oz) unsalted butter
150 g (5 oz) sugar
115 g (4 oz) light brown sugar
1 large egg
1 tsp vanilla essence
2½ tbsp cinnamon

In a bowl, sift the flour, baking soda and salt. In a large bowl, beat the butter, 50 g (2 oz) sugar and the brown sugar until well combined. Add the egg and vanilla, beating thoroughly. Stir in the sifted ingredients and mix well. Divide the dough in half and shape into logs. Wrap each log in clear film and refrigerate or freeze until firm.

In a small bowl, mix the remaining sugar with the cinnamon and spread on a plate. Unwrap the logs and roll them in cinnamon sugar until they are completely covered. Re-wrap the logs and refrigerate or freeze until firm.

Unwrap the logs and slice the dough 5 mm/¼ inch thick. Place the slices 2.5 cm/1 inch apart on a baking sheet and bake in a preheated oven at 180°C/350°F/Gas 4 for 10–12 minutes, or until golden. Put the biscuits on a rack to cool and bake the remaining slices. Serve cool.

KB

apple and blueberry tartlets with creamed raspberries

If you have difficulty getting blueberries then use any soft fruit in their place for the tartlets. The same goes for the raspberries in the sauce.

SERVES 4

FOR THE APPLE AND BLUEBERRY TARTLETS
225 g (8 oz) sweet pastry
25 g (1 oz) unsalted butter
25 g (1 oz) caster sugar
25 g (1 oz) ground hazelnuts
1 egg, lightly beaten
2 tsp plain flour
pinch of cinnamon
150 g (5 oz) blueberries
2 tbsp runny honey
2 Cox's apples, sliced 1 cm/½ inch thick

FOR THE CREAMED RASPBERRIES
150 ml (¼ pint) whipping cream
150 ml (¼ pint) milk
2 egg yolks
1 tbsp caster sugar
115 g (4 oz) raspberries, puréed
icing sugar, to dust

Roll out the pastry on a floured board until 5 mm/¼ inch thick, and use to line four 10 cm/4 inch size tartlet tins. Using a fork, prick the base of each tartlet and cover with clear film. Transfer to the refrigerator and leave to chill.

Place the butter and sugar in a bowl and cream until soft. Grind the hazelnuts in a blender and add to the sugar and butter mixture. Add 2 tbsp of the egg, all the flour and the cinnamon. Mix to combine thoroughly.

Place half the blueberries in a small bowl and crush lightly using the back of a spoon.

Remove the lined tartlet tins from the refrigerator, place them on a baking tray and spread the hazelnut mixture in each base. Spoon the crushed blueberries over the nut mixture and bake in a preheated oven at 220°C/425°F/Gas 7 for about 8 minutes.

Meanwhile, heat the honey in a medium frying pan, add the apple slices and cook over a medium heat, stirring occasionally, until golden and tender. Stir in the remaining blueberries and cook for a further minute.

Remove the tartlets from the oven and place on an upturned ramekin dish to release them from the tins. Replace the tartlets on the baking tin and bake for a further 4–5 minutes until golden.

Remove the tartlets from the oven and transfer to serving plates. Spoon the apple and blueberry mixture over the filling.

To make the creamed raspberry sauce: put the cream and milk in a saucepan and heat until just below boiling point.

Place the egg yolks in a medium bowl, add the sugar and beat together until smooth. Pour the hot cream mixture into the egg mixture, whisking continuously. Wipe out the pan and strain the custard back in. Cook over a low heat, whisking constantly until slightly thickened. Remove from the heat and add the raspberry purée; combine together and strain.

To serve, pour the raspberry cream around the tartlets and dust lightly with icing sugar.

KW

Cowboy cooks who picked up more saddle sores than they would care to admit.

summer **fruit crunch** slice

This pudding incorporates the lightest of cakes with the sweetest of summer fruits – topped with an 'explode in the mouth' crunchy topping. Use whatever soft summer fruits are available, but it is also really lovely with a selection of exotic fruits such as mango and passion fruits.

SERVES 4

3 eggs
150 g (5 oz) caster sugar
75 g (3 oz) plain flour
1½ tsp baking powder
pinch of salt
15 g (½ oz) unsalted butter
2 tbsp golden syrup
175 g (6 oz) mixed summer soft fruits
1 small glass Grand Marnier, Cointreau or kirsch
225 g (8 oz) crème fraîche

Whisk the eggs with 75 g (3 oz) of the caster sugar, until the mixture doubles in size. Sift the flour, ½ tsp of the baking powder and a pinch of salt onto the egg mixture. Using a metal spoon, cut all the dry ingredients into the egg mixture until blended. Transfer to a greaseproof paper-lined Swiss roll tin and bake for 8–10 minutes, in a preheated oven at 220°C/425°F/Gas 7, until golden and just cooked.

Put 50 g (2 oz) of the caster sugar, the unsalted butter and golden syrup in a pan and heat gently, stirring until the sugar dissolves. Increase the heat and cook without stirring until the mixture turns golden brown, then mix through 1 tsp baking powder. Pour the mixture onto a baking tray ensuring that it spreads evenly; cover with greaseproof paper and leave to cool.

Remove the cake from the oven, turn it out onto a surface which is lightly covered with caster sugar. Take off the paper and cut the cake into three pieces.

Mix the fruits with the liqueur and crème fraîche and cover the top of each cake with some of the fruit mixture.

Break the sugar honeycomb into small pieces and sprinkle over the fruit on the cake. Place the cakes on top of each other and serve.

KW

illustrated on previous pages

maple **pecan pie**

There are several grades of maple syrup and only the best will do for this pie. It is great served cold with a cup of tea, hot with custard as a dessert, or even with some fresh cinnamon ice-cream.

SERVES 8

23 cm/9-inch ready-made shortcrust pie shell
50 g (2 oz) unsalted butter
90 g (3½ oz) sugar
¼ tsp salt
3 large eggs
250 ml (8 fl oz) maple syrup
175 g (6 oz) toasted pecan pieces

Place the pie shell in a preheated oven at 140°C/275°F/Gas 1 to warm.

In a heatproof bowl, melt the butter over a pan of simmering water. Remove the bowl from the pan and add the sugar and salt. Stir until the butter is absorbed.

Beat in the eggs and maple syrup. Place the bowl back over the pan of simmering water, and stir the mixture until it is warm and glistening. Remove from the heat and add the pecans.

Pour the mixture into the warmed pie shell and bake for 45 minutes at 140°C/275°F/Gas 1 or until set. Set the pie on a rack to cool completely for several hours before serving.

KB

illustrated overleaf

SCOTLAND AND

Overlooking Calgary Bay on the Isle of Mull.

Scotland and Nova Scotia could not be more closely linked in personal terms; the fact is that present-day Nova Scotia holds on strongly to its Scottish roots. The folks there know the island and even the village their forefathers came from.

In the eighteenth century, the reasons for the disputes between England and Scotland were various and complex, but the centuries of disquiet eventually came to a head at the muddy field of Culloden in 1745. The English won the battle and it finally gave them a chance to put paid to the separation of the kingdoms and to join the two countries under English rule. Unfortunately that meant giving Scottish lands to English lords or lairds who decided that the best way to turn a penny from the soil was to get rid of the people and make way for sheep and a woollen industry. The Highland clearances began.

NOVA SCOTIA

Initially the Hebrides were spared the turmoil since they were already profitable with the kelp industry, sold as a fertilizer to the new wave of agriculture in Britain. However when the Napoleonic wars came to an end, the import duties were lifted, and there was an influx of cheap foreign goods and food. The kelp industry collapsed and now even the Hebrides had to be handed over to sheep to make a profit. Whole islands and villages were cleared and sent packing for the new

Eugene de Blanc explains the finer points of fly fishing.

Big Kevin had to substitute bin liners and duct tape for waders as we couldn't find any big enough to fit him.

Fly fishing on the Magaree River in Nova Scotia, during the 'Fall'.

worlds of Canada, America, Australia and New Zealand.

For those who were sent, it was hard work, and for those who stayed, there was worse to come. The famine of 1846, following the failure of the potato crop, meant that many decided voluntarily to set sail for the promised land. What these families took with them, other than a very few possessions, was the Gaelic language, music and, of course, recipes, none of which were written down.

What they found in Nova Scotia, in places such as Cape Breton, was a land that was poor and a sea that was teeming with fish. They ended up trading salt cod with the West Indies and got in return molasses and spices such as pepper and ginger. Blackstrap molasses had originally been bought to feed cattle during the winter but, with little else for variety, these new settlers used it to create new recipes. Today molasses is as common as salt and pepper: it can be found on every table and in every larder of those Scottish descendants in Cape Breton.

tobermory cheese, **potato** and **turnip soufflé**

This makes a wonderful starter or main course when served with haggis.

SERVES 8 AS A STARTER,
4 AS A MAIN COURSE

- 900 g (2 lb) potatoes, peeled
- 900 g (2 lb) turnips, peeled and cut into small pieces
- 50 g (2 oz) butter
- 50 g (2 oz) plain flour
- 600 ml (1 pint) milk
- pinch of nutmeg
- 50 g (2 oz) Tobermory cheese (or Cheddar will do), grated
- 3 eggs, separated
- salt and freshly ground black pepper

In separate pans, cook the potatoes and turnips in boiling salted water for 20 minutes. Drain and mash both together, ensuring that there are no lumps and that they are well mixed.

Melt the butter in a saucepan and stir in the flour, cook for 2 minutes to form a roux. Gradually add the milk, stirring constantly until a thick smooth sauce is developed. Season with salt, pepper and nutmeg. Stir in half of the cheese.

Stir the egg yolks into the potatoes. Whisk the egg whites until they form soft peaks and gently fold into the potatoes. Spoon into 8 ramekin dishes or a large ovenproof dish. Sprinkle the remaining cheese on top and bake in a preheated oven at 200°C/400°F/Gas 6 for 20 minutes, until well risen and golden brown.

KW

Great cheese from Sgriob-Ruadh farm, Mull.

smoked haddock and spring onion soup

If ever there was a case for using only the finest ingredients it's with this fish. I can understand why those who have never tasted the naturally smoked variety might be tempted to spend their hard-earned cash on the bright yellow dyed version. Don't – go for the pale, naturally smoked fish and experience the difference in flavour.

SERVES 6

350 g (12 oz) potatoes, diced
50 g (2 oz) butter
50 g (2 oz) onions, finely chopped
450g (1 lb) Finnan smoked haddock fillets
300 ml (½ pint) water
600 ml (1 pint) milk
75 g (3 oz) spring onions, green only, finely shredded
50 ml (2 fl oz) whipping cream
salt and freshly ground white pepper

Cook the potatoes in a pan of salted boiling water until just cooked, about 20 minutes. Meanwhile, melt half of the butter in a large pan, add the onions and cook without colouring until soft.

Cut the smoked haddock fillets into large pieces and add them to the onions. Pour the water into the pan and bring to the boil; reduce the heat and simmer for about 10 minutes until the fish is cooked through. Transfer the fish onto a dish and, when cool enough to handle, break into pieces, discarding any skin and bones. Reserve the cooking liquor.

Drain the potatoes, leave in the pan over a low heat for a minute to dry, and mash until smooth. Add the remaining butter and season with salt and white pepper.

Slowly incorporate the cooking liquor into the mashed potato and mix thoroughly. Stir in the milk, bring to the boil, cover and simmer for 3–4 minutes. Add the flaked fish, spring onions and cream, adjust the seasoning and serve.

KW

onion and smoked salmon tart

I eat this when I'm not sure what I'm going to eat next. It is light and doesn't leave you with that heavy feeling. Or you can serve this before something big, such as the country elk steak.

SERVES 4

FOR THE TART
115 g (4 oz) flour
pinch of salt
¼ tsp sugar
75 g (3 oz) unsalted butter, cut up
2½ tbsp ice water

FOR THE TOPPING
1 large onion, thinly sliced
1 large egg yolk with ½ tsp water
3 tbsp sour cream, softened
115 g (4 oz) smoked salmon, cut into thin strips
1 tbsp chopped parsley
1 tsp chopped dill
1 tbsp fresh lemon juice
salt and freshly ground black pepper

Make the pastry; in a food processor, combine the flour, salt and sugar. Add the butter and mix until the mixture resembles coarse breadcrumbs. Add the ice water and process until the pastry comes together. Use more water if needed. On a lightly floured surface, shape into a round disc, wrap in clear film and refrigerate until chilled. (Pastry will keep for 2 days in the refrigerator.)

On a lightly floured piece of parchment paper, roll out the pastry to a 33 cm/13 inch round; place the pastry and parchment on a baking sheet.

Place the onion slices on the pastry round in a single layer, stopping 2.5 cm/1 inch from the edge. Season with salt and pepper. Fold the edge of the pastry over onto the onion and brush the rim with the egg wash. Bake in a preheated oven at 230°C/450°F/Gas 8 for 20 minutes until golden. Let cool.

With a warm fork, stir the sour cream and drizzle over the tart. Arrange the smoked salmon on the tart. Sprinkle the parsley, dill, and lemon juice over the top and serve.

KB

seared scallops on a parsnip purée

The key to this dish is fresh scallops, which are very, very lightly cooked and perfectly seasoned. The parsnip purée should be very light, so do beat it hard with a wooden spoon prior to putting the cream in.

SERVES 6

450 g (1 lb) parsnips, peeled and cubed
24 scallops
175 g (6 oz) unsalted butter
175 ml (6 fl oz) whipping cream
450 ml (¾ pint) fish stock
300 ml (½ pint) dry vermouth
50 g (2 oz) shallots, finely diced
1 bay leaf
vegetable oil, for frying
50 g (2 oz) carrots, finely shredded into long thin strips
50 g (2 oz) leek, shredded to the same size as the carrots
zest of 1 lemon, finely shredded into long thin strips
75 g (3 oz) streaky bacon, diced
25 g (1 oz) chives, finely snipped
salt and freshly ground black pepper

Cook the parsnips in a pan of boiling salted water. Meanwhile shell, trim and clean the scallops. Detach the roe (coral) and slice the flesh into two discs.

Drain the parsnips and return to a low heat, to remove any excess moisture. Remove from heat and add 25 g (l oz) of the butter and 50 ml (2 fl oz) of the cream and season with salt and black pepper.

Start the sauce by bringing the stock, vermouth, shallots and bay leaf to the boil, reduce the heat slightly and allow to reduce to a syrupy consistency.

Meanwhile, in a deep saucepan heat sufficient oil to shallow fry the vegetables and lemon zest. Once the oil is hot, add the vegetables and lemon zest and cook until they colour. Remove and leave to drain on kitchen paper. Dry fry the bacon until just turning crisp and also drain on paper.

Remove the reduced stock from the heat and slowly add the rest of the cream. Slowly whisk in small amounts of the remaining butter, ensuring that it blends with the other ingredients to make a smooth sauce. Add the snipped chives and season to taste. Strain the sauce into a small jug.

Season the scallops and roe with salt and black pepper. Lightly grease a griddle pan and heat. Quickly cook the scallops for no longer than 40 seconds on each side. To serve, place a mound of parsnip purée in the centre of each plate and sprinkle with bacon. Put a portion of scallops on top and cap with the fried vegetables. Spoon a little of the sauce and place the roes around the outside of dish.

KW

spiced kipper pâté with a lemon grass and ginger salad

The Liverpool comedian Stan Boardman once told me that he hated kippers because they were 'big headed buggers with no guts'! Yes, laughter is good for you, and so are kippers. As for the salad, the infusion of ginger and lemon grass in good quality oil, will add a lovely dimension to it. I always make a reasonable quantity and bottle it, as it has such a wide variety of uses.

SERVES 6

400 g (14 oz) kippers, skinned and boned
2 eggs (1 separated)
juice of 1 lemon
4 tbsp dry white wine
pinch of paprika
½ tsp turmeric
3 red chillies, deseeded and finely diced
90 ml (3 fl oz) whipping cream
90 ml (3 fl oz) extra-virgin olive oil
5 mm (¼ inch) of fresh ginger root, peeled and diced
½ stick lemon grass, finely chopped
2 tbsp sherry vinegar
175 g (6 oz) mixed baby leaves
salt and freshly ground black pepper

Place the kipper flesh in a food processor and blend until smooth. Season with salt, add 1 egg white and blend again for approximately 1 minute until very smooth. For best results press the mixture through a sieve into a bowl which is resting over a larger bowl containing ice.

Add the remaining egg yolk and whole egg, then the lemon juice, white wine, paprika, turmeric and diced chillies. Gradually beat in the cream, taking great care not to overbeat the mixture as this will curdle the cream. Season with salt and freshly ground black pepper.

Transfer the mixture into 6 lightly buttered ramekins, ensuring that the mixture is pressed firmly down with a metal spoon. Cover each ramekin with lightly buttered paper and cook in a preheated oven at 200°C/400°F/Gas 6 for 15–18 minutes.

Gently warm the olive oil in a small pan, add the ginger and lemon grass and leave off the heat to infuse for 10 minutes, then strain. Add the vinegar and seasoning to the olive oil and use to dress the salad leaves.

To serve, place a mound of salad leaves high on each plate, remove pâtés from the ramekins and sit them on the leaves.

KW

salt cod cakes with tarragon mayonnaise

I am still trying to decide if I like the cod cakes or the mayo better!

MAKES 8–10

FOR THE MAYONNAISE

225 g (8 oz) mayonnaise
2 tbsp chopped fresh tarragon
1 tbsp chopped chives

FOR THE COD CAKES

450 g (1 lb) skinless salt cod fillets
750 ml (1¼ pints) milk
4 medium potatoes, diced
5 tbsp whipping cream
75 g (3 oz) spring onions, thinly sliced
2 tbsp chopped fresh tarragon
1 tbsp chopped parsley
2 tbsp olive oil
115 g (4 oz) flour
vegetable oil, for frying
salt and freshly ground black pepper

In a bowl, mix the mayonnaise, tarragon and chives. Cover and refrigerate until ready to serve.

In a bowl, cover the salt cod with water and soak overnight in the refrigerator. Drain and flake the salt cod and place in large saucepan. Add the milk and simmer over a medium heat for 10 minutes. The cod should flake easily when done. Drain the cod and place in a large bowl.

In a medium saucepan, cover the potatoes with water and boil until tender, about 10 minutes. Drain the potatoes and allow to cool. Add the potatoes to the cod along with the cream, spring onions, tarragon, parsley and olive oil.

Season with salt and ground pepper to taste. Stir well to combine ingredients and shape into 7.5 cm/3 inch cakes about 2 cm/¾ inch thick. Lightly dust cakes with flour and set them on a plate.

Heat 1 cm/½ inch vegetable oil in a frying pan and fry the cod cakes, turning once, until golden brown and crisp. Drain on kitchen paper and keep warm while you cook the other cakes. Serve with the tarragon mayonnaise.

KB

salt cod with curds

This is a very traditional Nova Scotia recipe that we saw Helen MacNeil make. Like many old recipes it is true comfort food. It is actually supposed to use leftovers, but Helen says they like it so much that they always cook extra salt cod so they can make this the next day. It is usually served with traditional curds, gently cooked on the stove top in the kitchen.

SERVES 4

225 g (8 oz) butter
350 g (12 oz) waxy potatoes, cooked with their skins on, then peeled and cut into 1 cm/½ inch cubes
225 g (8 oz) left-over salt cod, soaked overnight then boiled
salt and freshly ground black pepper
curds or cottage cheese, to serve
pickled beetroot, to serve
Buttermilk Biscuits (see page 116), to serve

Place a large heavy pan on a high heat, melt the butter, then gradually add the potato, which should stick to the bottom of the pan and brown, scrape this off with a spoon or spatula but do not allow it to burn as this will make the dish bitter. Cook for several minutes until all of the potato is nicely heated through and soft.

Flake the salt cod, add to the potato and heat. Season with plenty of pepper and some salt depending on how salty the fish is.

Serve with curds or cottage cheese, pickled beetroot and the Buttermilk Biscuits.

KB

lobster **risotto**

The richness of the lobster goes so well with the rice, and the addition of some truffle sauce as a condiment makes this a top class dish for special occasions.

SERVES 3–4

4 tbsp brandy
3 tbsp tomato purée
½ tsp red pepper flakes
2 lobsters, steamed and meat diced
3 tbsp olive oil
1 large onion, chopped
1 tsp very finely chopped garlic
200 g (7 oz) arborio rice
1 litre (1¾ pints) clam juice
freshly ground black pepper
grated Parmesan cheese, to serve

In a bowl, combine the brandy, tomato purée and red pepper flakes. Stir in the cooked lobster, cover and refrigerate for 2 hours.

Heat the oil in a medium saucepan and cook the onion and garlic until tender. Add the rice and stir until warm. Add the clam juice, about one quarter at a time and stir. Continue to add the clam juice only as long as the rice will absorb it. This may take 25–30 minutes. The rice should be almost al dente. Add the lobster mixture and cook until heated through and rice is al dente. Season with ground black pepper and serve with the grated Parmesan.

KB

wild salmon in a molasses crab-apple sauce

A very unusual combination that you won't believe until you've tried it. The sweetness of the molasses combines with the tartness of the crab-apples to produce a very delicate sweet and sour flavour, with the earthy richness of the molasses.

SERVES 2

115 (4 oz) butter
2 wild salmon steaks
115 (4 oz) crab-apples, cored and cut into 1 cm (½ inch) cubes
185 g (6½ oz) molasses
salt and freshly ground black pepper

Place a heavy, dry frying pan on the stove to heat. Take a small knob of the butter and spread thinly on both sides of the salmon steaks (if you can't get wild salmon you might not have to butter the steaks depending on how fatty your fish is, farmed salmon tends to be a bit fattier than wild), then season them with salt and pepper.

When the pan is very hot, add the steaks. These will need turning after only a few minutes depending on heat of the pan and thickness of the steaks. To test them, press with the back of a spoon, when they are just springy to the touch they are done.

Meanwhile, in a small saucepan, melt the remainder of the butter. Add the crab-apples and gently sauté for just 1 minute. (If you can't get crab-apples, use cooking apples and add a little lemon juice since crab-apples are quite sour.) They should not be allowed to get soft. Add the molasses; bring to a simmer and simmer for 1 more minute.

Serve on top of the salmon steaks.

KB

breast of chicken in a tomato and langoustine confit

This is a great dish for those special family celebrations, as chicken is a great favourite with most family members and even grandma and grandpa are able to chew it!

SERVES 4

1 tbsp olive oil
50 g (2 oz) unsalted butter
4 skinless chicken breasts
12 shallots, peeled
2 cloves garlic, crushed
50 g (2 oz) lardons (small pieces of bacon)
½ tbsp chopped fresh tarragon
175 g (6 oz) langoustines
50 g (2 oz) chestnut mushrooms, sliced
450 g (1 1b) plum tomatoes, skinned, deseeded and diced
120 ml (4 fl oz) tomato juice
2 tbsp sun-dried tomato purée
1 glass dry white wine
2 tbsp torn basil
4 portions fresh spinach
salt and freshly ground black pepper

Heat the olive oil and butter in a pan; season the chicken breasts with salt and black pepper and add them to the pan. Cook gently without excessive colouring. Remove from the pan, cover and keep warm.

Place the shallots, garlic, bacon and tarragon in the same pan. Cook for 4 minutes and then add the langoustines, mushrooms and chopped tomatoes. Cook gently for 2 minutes. Add the tomato juice, tomato purée, white wine and season with salt and black pepper and bring to the boil. Add the torn basil to the tomato sauce and turn off the heat.

In a large pan, wilt the spinach and season with salt and black pepper.

To serve, cut each chicken breast into 4 slices. Place a mound of spinach on each plate and arrange the chicken over the spinach. Spoon a little of the sauce over the chicken, placing a langoustine on top. Pour the remaining sauce around the plate.

KW

pan fried **haddock** with cucumber sauce

Be sure the oil is very hot when frying, so your fish has a crispy coating.

SERVES 6

115 g (4 oz) flour
6 haddock fillets
1 egg
4 tbsp milk
vegetable oil, for frying
salt and freshly ground black pepper
whole chives, to garnish
lemon wedges, to serve

FOR THE CUCUMBER SAUCE
1 cucumber, peeled and chopped
1 onion, roughly chopped
2 tbsp chopped fresh parsley
2 tbsp vegetable oil
4 tbsp red wine vinegar

Make the sauce; in a food processor or blender add the cucumber, onion and parsley. Process until finely chopped. Add the oil and vinegar and process until well blended. Chill until ready to serve.

In a bowl, season the flour with 1 tsp salt and ½ tsp black pepper. Dry the haddock fillets and season lightly with salt and pepper. Beat the egg in a bowl then add the milk, stirring to mix together.

Dip the haddock fillets into the seasoned flour to coat well, shaking off the excess. Then dip into the egg mixture, then in the flour coating a second time.

Fry the fish in the vegetable oil over a high heat for 6–8 minutes until it has a golden crust and is flaky. Garnish with whole chives and serve with the cucumber sauce and lemon wedges.

KB

peppered beef with braised cabbage and griddled scallops

A wonderful dish which is very rich and will satisfy even the biggest appetites.

SERVES 4

25 g (1 oz) dried porcini mushrooms
1 glass Madeira or sherry
4 x 175 g (6 oz) fillet steaks, trimmed
4 tbsp crushed black peppercorns
450 g (1 lb) spring cabbage, finely shredded
900 ml (1½ pints) hot chicken stock
vegetable oil, for roasting
12 scallops with roe attached
1 cube fresh ginger root, grated
4 tbsp extra-virgin olive oil
2 tbsp finely chopped dill
3 tomatoes, peeled, deseeded and finely chopped
175 g (6 oz) butter, chilled
50 g (2 oz) Mâcon ham or prosciutto, finely diced
¼ tsp cumin
salt and freshly ground black pepper

illustrated overleaf

Soak the porcini mushrooms in the Madeira. Roll the fillet steaks in the crushed peppercorns and season with a little salt. Cook the cabbage in the boiling chicken stock with a little salt.

Heat a little oil in a roasting dish. Seal the beef on all sides and cook in a preheated oven at 220°C/425°F/Gas 7 for 15–20 minutes depending on how you like your beef to be cooked.

Remove the roes from the scallops and cut into thick slices, place to one side.

Mix together the grated ginger and 1 tablespoon of the dill with the extra-virgin olive oil and add a little salt. Brush the oil over the scallops, cover and place to one side.

Add the remaining dill to the diced tomato flesh, mix in ½ tbsp of the ginger oil and a little salt and pepper.

Drain the cabbage, retaining the cooking liquid in a pan. Replace the pan of stock over a high heat and reduce by half, adding the Madeira which was used to soak the porcini mushrooms.

Heat 50 g (2 oz) butter in a large pan, add the cabbage, dice the porcini and add to the pan, followed by the Mâcon ham. Season with salt, pepper and cumin. Add the sliced scallop roe and carefully mix through.

Transfer the cabbage mixture into 4 lightly buttered dariole moulds, cover and place into the oven.

continued opposite

Remove the beef, turn off the heat, cover and place to one side.

Heat a griddle pan. Place the scallops on the hot griddle and cook for 15–20 seconds on both sides. Remove from the heat.

For the sauce, whisk the remaining butter into the reduced chicken stock, check the seasoning and adjust if necessary.

To serve, unmould the cabbage onto the centre of each plate. Slice the beef and arrange it, overlapping over the cabbage. Place 3 small spoonfuls of the tomato and dill mixture around the plate and place a scallop on each. Drizzle a little sauce around the plate and serve.

KW

sweet **molasses chicken**

Molasses is truly underrated in everyday cooking, Louisiana is about the only American state still producing it, but down here it is used in cakes, pralines etc. Since going to Nova Scotia I've used it in lots of dishes. It is sweet and rich all in one and for this dish it is perfect. I love sweet and spicy, add more mustard for a tangier taste.

SERVES 4

3 lb chicken, cut in pieces
185 g (6½ oz) molasses
4 cloves garlic, very finely chopped
2 tbsp Dijon mustard
1 onion, thinly sliced
1 tbsp vegetable oil
salt and freshly ground black pepper

Season the chicken with salt and pepper to taste. In a bowl, mix the molasses, mustard, garlic and onion. Dip chicken into mixture and coat well.

Place chicken pieces in an oiled roasting tin. Any extra molasses mixture can be spooned over the chicken before or after cooking. Cover and bake in a preheated oven at 190°C/375°F/Gas 5 for 40 minutes, until the chicken is done.

KB

pot roasted **highland beef** with **root vegetables** and ginger glaze

Traditional methods of cooking large joints of beef do, in my opinion, produce the best results. Lots of lovely fresh vegetables gently cooked alongside the meat yield a wealth of flavours.

SERVES 4–6

900 g (2 lb) top or silverside beef
2 cloves garlic, chopped
3 tbsp oil
300 ml (½ pint) red wine
600 ml (1 pint) brown veal or beef stock
150 ml (¼ pint) tomato juice or l tbsp tomato purée
2 bay leaves
2–3 sprigs each of thyme and rosemary
150 g (5 oz) button onions
2–4 carrots
2–4 small turnips
2–4 small parsnips
1 large leek
1 small swede
1 tbsp mustard
2–3 tbsp ginger preserves, or chopped stem ginger with syrup
salt and freshly ground black pepper
fresh herbs, to garnish

Season the beef with salt, pepper and rub with garlic. Heat half the oil in a heavy casserole and brown the beef all over until a crust is formed (it takes about 10 minutes).

Pour off the fat and add the wine. Boil to reduce to half and then half cover the meat with the stock; check the seasoning. Add the tomato juice or purée, bay leaves, thyme and rosemary. Bring to the boil, skim and cover. Braise slowly in a preheated oven at 200°C/400°F/Gas 6 for 1¾–2 hours, until tender.

Meanwhile, cut the vegetables into small chunks and brown lightly in the rest of the oil. Add the vegetables to the casserole and finish cooking in the oven, uncovered, until the meat and vegetables are tender, about another 45–60 minutes. About 15 minutes before the end of the cooking time, take the casserole out of the oven and smear the top of the meat with the mustard and spoon the ginger preserves over the meat. This will glaze in the oven during the rest of the cooking time.

To serve, transfer the meat and vegetables to a serving platter; garnish with fresh herbs. Skim off the excess fat from the cooking liquor, correct the colour, seasoning and consistency of the sauce by boiling it down to thicken (alternatively, you can thicken it with cornflour diluted with a little water). Strain the sauce and serve separately.

KW

lavender and ginger ice cream

The use of lavender in cooking is not widespread and it is important to be aware of certain factors. Most importantly, you must be sure that the flowers have not been sprayed with pesticides. The sprigs can be used fresh, usually between June and July, or dried at other times of the year. If using dried lavender, be sparing with the amount, as too much will ruin the dish. The aim is to achieve a subtlety of flavour, it should not overpower the dish. However, get it right and oh! what a wonderful taste!

SERVES 4–6

6 large egg yolks
50 g (2 oz) caster sugar
4 cm (1½ inches) fresh ginger root, finely chopped
4 sprigs lavender
600 ml (1 pint) whipping cream
10 tbsp runny honey

In a bowl whisk the egg yolks and sugar until light and fluffy.

Place the ginger in a pan with the lavender and cream and bring to the boil. Pour the hot cream onto the egg mixture and mix together. Return the mixture to the pan and heat over a low heat stirring continuously or the mixture will curdle. Once the mixture has developed enough body to coat the back of the spoon, add the honey and strain into a clean bowl.

If you are lucky enough to own an ice cream machine, then have a rest whilst the machine takes over! If not, transfer the mixture into a shallow dish, cover with clear film and place in the freezer. You will need to stir the ice cream every 20 minutes until it sets.

KW

lemon ice box pie

Of all the desserts my mother made for me, this was my favourite. I would butter a knife, so it cut through the meringue smoothly and sit with my slice of pie for 30 minutes enjoying every bite. So my tip is take your time with this one, don't rush a crumb of it.

SERVES 8

FOR THE CRUST
115 g (4 oz) Graham crackers, crushed*
175 g (6 oz) flour
200 g (7 oz) sugar
115 g (4 oz) unsalted butter, cut up
2 large eggs, lightly beaten

FOR THE FILLING AND TOPPING
2 large eggs, separated
¼ tsp cream of tartar
50 g (2 oz) sugar
225 g (8 oz) condensed milk
120 ml (4 fl oz) fresh lemon juice

Make the crust; in a large bowl, stir together the Graham cracker crumbs, flour and sugar. Add the butter and blend until the mixture resembles coarse breadcrumbs. Add the lightly beaten eggs to the crumb mixture, blending with a fork. Press the mixture evenly into a 22.5 cm/9 inch pie dish.

Make the meringue topping. In a bowl, have the egg whites at room temperature. Add the cream of tartar and sugar. Beat the egg whites until stiff using a whisk.

Make the filling; in a bowl, blend the condensed milk, lemon juice and egg yolks. Pour the mixture into the pie crust. Top with the meringue and bake in preheated oven at 160°C/325°F/Gas 3 for about 15 minutes or until the meringue has browned. Cool on a rack, chill and serve.

*If you cannot find Graham crackers use ginger nuts or Digestive biscuits.

KB

buttermilk pie

You might need to get to know a local dairy farmer, because if you can use fresh, home-made butter and buttermilk, this pie turns out sensational. If you never knew your great-grandmother, this pie will get you very close.

SERVES 8

FOR THE CRUST
115 g (4 oz) Graham crackers, crushed*
175 g (6 oz) flour
200 g (7 oz) sugar
115 g (4 oz) butter, unsalted, cut up
2 large eggs, lightly beaten

FOR THE FILLING
115 g (4 oz) butter
400 g (14 oz) sugar
3 tbsp flour
3 large eggs, beaten
250 ml (8 fl oz) buttermilk
1 tsp vanilla essence
pinch of ground nutmeg

Make the crust; in a large bowl, stir together the Graham cracker crumbs, flour and sugar. Add the butter and blend until the mixture resembles coarse breadcrumbs. Add the eggs to the crumb mixture, blending with a fork. Press the mixture evenly into the bottom of a 22.5 cm/9 inch pie dish.

Make the filling: cream together the butter and sugar until smooth. Add the flour and eggs, and beat well. Stir in the buttermilk, vanilla and nutmeg. Pour the mixture into the pie shell. Bake in a preheated 180°C/350°F/Gas 4 oven for 45–50 minutes. Let the pie cool on a rack in the pan, slice and serve.

*If you cannot find Graham crackers use ginger nuts or Digestive biscuits.

KB

butterscotch tart with a whisky and honey cream

The combination of flavours in this recipe make it a sheer delight to cook, so why not enjoy yourself and treat your family and friends at the same time.

SERVES 6

200 g (7 oz) plain flour
90 g (3½ oz) unsalted butter, chilled and cubed
2–3 tbsp cold water
1 small can evaporated milk, chilled
175 g (6 oz) light muscovado sugar
1 measure of whisky
2 tbsp honey
50 g (2 oz) stem ginger, diced
250 ml (8 fl oz) clotted cream
icing sugar, for dusting
6 small mint leaves, to decorate

Place the flour in a food processor, add the butter and blend until the mixture resembles fine breadcrumbs. Add the cold water and blend for 30 seconds.

Remove from the processor and place on a lightly floured pastry board. Gently form the pastry into a smooth ball and roll out. Grease a 20 cm/8 inch flan ring and line the flan ring with the pastry. Cover with greaseproof paper and fill with baking beans. Cook in a preheated oven at 200°C/400°F/Gas 6 for 18–20 minutes.

Whisk together the evaporated milk and sugar until the mixture becomes pale in colour and quite thick. Remove the baking beans and paper from the flan ring and pour the mixture over the pastry. Bake in the oven for 10 minutes. Allow the tart to cool and remove from the flan ring.

Add the whisky, honey and ginger to the clotted cream and mix through.

To serve, place a slice of the flan on a plate and dust with icing sugar. Place a neat spoonful of clotted cream to one side, topped with a single mint leaf.

KW

molasses cake or hot water gingerbread

After Helen MacNeil's salt cod with fresh curds and a singalong in the living room, she went to the kitchen and returned with steaming bowls of this wonderful dessert. The banana sauce was J. Edgar's idea. (We blessed our producer Andrew with this name after sharing many meals together watching him Hoover up his food.)

SERVES 8

FOR THE CAKE
75 g (3 oz) margarine or shortening
115 g (4 oz) brown sugar
1 egg, well beaten
375 g (13 oz) dark molasses
225 g (8 oz) sifted plain flour
1 tsp ground ginger
1 tsp cinnamon
¼ tsp ground nutmeg
¼ tsp cloves
½ tsp salt
1½ tsp baking soda
250 ml (8 fl oz) hot water
whipping cream, to serve

FOR THE TOPPING
3 apples, peeled and sliced
115 g (4 oz) brown sugar
knob of butter, cut up

FOR THE SPICY BANANA SAUCE
115 (4 oz) peeled sliced bananas
juice of 1 lemon
50 g (2 oz) molasses
2 tsp cardamom seeds
vanilla essence
4 tsp dark rum
50 g (2 oz) sugar

In a large bowl, cream together the margarine and sugar until fluffy. Add the beaten egg and molasses and blend well.

Sift the flour with the spices, salt and baking soda together three times and gradually add to the creamed mixture alternately with the hot water, beating the mix until smooth after each addition of flour.

Line a 45 x 30 cm/18 x 12 inch dish with parchment paper, and arrange the topping of apples, sugar and butter in the bottom of the dish. Spoon the molasses cake mixture into the dish and bake in a preheated oven at 180°C/350°F/Gas 4 for 50 minutes.

Meanwhile, make the sauce: toss the sliced banana in the lemon juice, place in a saucepan with the molasses, cardamom, vanilla, rum and sugar and bring to boil and simmer for 10 minutes. Pass through a fine sieve.

Serve the molasses cake hot, straight from the pan, with the sauce and with whipping cream.

KB

fig pudding

This is a gorgeous but very naughty pudding – one of my favourites! I like to serve my Lavender and Ginger Ice Cream with this recipe (see page 149).

SERVES 6

25 g (1 oz) self-raising flour
175 g (6 oz) white breadcrumbs
115 g (4 oz) shredded suet
225 g (8 oz) dates, pitted and chopped
150 g (5 oz) dried figs, roughly chopped
115 g (4 oz) raisins
50 g (2 oz) preserved ginger, finely chopped
½ tsp mixed spices
pinch of cinnamon
grated zest and juice of 1 orange
2 large eggs, beaten
50 ml (2 fl oz) sherry

In a large bowl, mix together the flour, breadcrumbs and suet. Add the fruit, spices and orange zest and mix together. Make a well in the centre and pour in the beaten eggs, sherry and orange juice, mixing to form a batter.

Pour the mixture into a buttered 900 ml (1½ pint) pudding basin and cover first with greaseproof paper, and top with aluminium foil. Place the basin in a steamer and cook for 4 hours.

To serve, place a portion on a large plate with a large slice of lavender and ginger ice cream. Or place a portion in a large soup bowl and flood the bowl with custard.

KW

spiced **treacle loaf**

This is a lovely deep, rich loaf which eats beautifully with cheese or simply as a stand alone dish. Like many of this type of loaf, it will actually improve after a couple of days, but it never lasts that long in my house.

MAKES A 450 G (1 LB) LOAF

75 g (3 oz) black treacle
50 g (2 oz) muscovado sugar
½ tsp cinnamon
½ tsp ground mixed spices
pinch of freshly grated nutmeg
225 g (8 oz) plain flour, sifted
25 g (1 oz) currants
75 g (3 oz) sultanas
zest of 1 lemon
50 g (2 oz) unsalted butter, melted
5 tbsp milk
1 egg
cheese, to serve

Cream the treacle and sugar together until well blended. In a separate bowl, add the spices and lemon zest to the flour, mix through and add to the treacle mixture. Add the dried fruit and then mix in the melted butter, milk and egg to form a thick batter.

Transfer the mixture to a lined 450 g (1 lb) loaf tin and cook in a preheated oven at 180°C/350°F/Gas 4 for 35 minutes. The loaf should not be overcooked as it eats best when slightly moist.

Serve with cheese.

KW

apple **gingerbread**

Grab this – and a cup of coffee – for a quick breakfast when you are running late.

SERVES 8

15 g (4 oz) butter
2 eggs, beaten
115 g (4 oz) light brown sugar
225 g (8 oz) plain flour
2 tbsp baking powder
2 tbsp ground ginger
1 tbsp ground cinnamon
¼ tsp salt
185 g (6½ oz) molasses
120 ml (4 fl oz) sour cream
2 apples, peeled, cored and diced

In a bowl, place the butter and slowly add the beaten eggs and sugar, mixing until smooth. In a different bowl, mix the flour, baking powder, ginger, cinnamon and salt thoroughly. In a cup, stir together the molasses and sour cream. Alternately add a little of the flour mixture and the molasses mixture to the creamed butter, mixing thoroughly, until they are all absorbed.

Core, peel and dice the apples. Sprinkle flour lightly over the apples and fold into the mixture.

Transfer the mixture to a greased pan and bake in a preheated oven at 180°C/350°F/Gas 4 for 45 minutes.

KB

hot **raspberry** and **chocolate pudding** with a white chocolate sauce and summer fruit compote

This is one of the sexiest puddings around, but be sure to adhere to the cooking times. The pudding should be firm on the outside yet still a little runny on the inside.

SERVES 6

FOR THE CHOCOLATE PUDDING
90 g (3½ oz) unsalted butter
90 g (3½ oz) good quality dark chocolate, chopped into small pieces
3 large eggs
3 large egg yolks
75 g (3 oz) castor sugar
15 g (½ oz) plain flour
18 raspberries
icing sugar, to dust
6 small sprigs of mint, to decorate

FOR THE WHITE CHOCOLATE SAUCE
4 large egg yolks
40 g (1½ oz) caster sugar
450 ml (¾ pint) milk
40 g (1½ oz) good quality white chocolate, chopped into small pieces.

FOR THE COMPOTE OF SUMMER FRUITS
50 g (2 oz) strawberries, quartered
50 g (2 oz) raspberries
25 g (1 oz) blackcurrants
1 tbsp lavender honey

Prepare the white chocolate sauce; in a bowl, whisk the egg yolks and sugar together until light and fluffy. Heat the milk until it boils and pour slowly onto the egg and sugar mixture, stirring to ensure that it is incorporated. Transfer the mixture back into the pan and heat gently, stirring with a wooden spoon, until the mixture gains enough body to coat the back of the spoon. Add the white chocolate pieces to the sauce and mix thoroughly. Remove the sauce from the heat, allow to cool and chill until ready to serve.

To make the chocolate pudding, lightly butter six 150 ml (¼ pint) ramekins and line the bases with greaseproof paper. Melt the butter in a pan over a low heat. Add the dark chocolate pieces, remove from the heat and stir until the chocolate melts. In a bowl, whisk together the 3 eggs, the 3 egg yolks and the sugar, until the mixture becomes thick. Whisk in the chocolate mixture, then slowly whisk in the flour.

Half-fill the ramekins with the chocolate mixture, place 3 raspberries on top and top up with the rest of the mixture, so that the raspberries are in the centre. Bake in a preheated oven at 180°C/350°F/Gas 4 for 15 minutes or until set. Meanwhile, make the the compote of fruit; in a pan, mix together all the ingredients and gently warm over a low heat until the fruit breaks down.

To serve, remove the puddings from the ramekins and place in the centre of each plate, dust with icing sugar. Flood the plates with the sauce and place 3 spoonfuls of the compote around the pudding. Decorate with a sprig of mint.

KW

spiced **chocolate pudding** with cherry compote

The blend of cherries and chocolate in this pudding is a gastronomic marriage made in heaven.

SERVES 6

25 g (1 oz) butter
50 g (2 oz) plus 1 tbsp light muscovado sugar
115 g (4 oz) brioche or sliced bread, cut into 1 cm (½ inch) cubes
3 eggs
175 ml (6 fl oz) milk
175 ml (6 fl oz) whipping cream
2 tbsp rum
pinch of ground cinnamon
pinch of ground nutmeg
pinch of ground ginger
pinch of salt
40 g (1½ oz) dried sour cherries (optional)
115 g (4 oz) dark chocolate, chopped
150 ml (¼ pint) sauce Anglaise
melted chocolate or sauce (optional)
whipped cream or ice cream (optional)
4 sprigs mint, to decorate
cinnamon flavoured icing sugar, to decorate

FOR THE CHERRY COMPOTE
350 g (12 oz) canned pitted sour cherries
2 tbsp cornflour
25 g (1 oz) caster sugar
2 tbsp kirsch or rum (optional)

Butter six 100 ml (3½ fl oz) ramekin dishes and coat with 1 tbsp of the sugar. Put the bread cubes into a large bowl.

Beat together the sugar, eggs, milk, cream, rum, spices and salt. If using the dried cherries, place them on the bread and then pour the mixture over. Leave to stand for 10 minutes to enable the bread to soak up the mixture, and then stir in the chocolate.

Spoon the mixture into the buttered ramekins and place them in a roasting tin. Pour enough hot water to reach halfway up the sides of the ramekins. Bake in a preheated oven at 150°C/300°F/Gas 2 or 160°C/325°F/Gas 3 for about 30 minutes.

Make the cherry compote; strain the cherries from the juice and reserve. Moisten the cornflour with a little cherry juice. Put the rest of the cherry juice in a pan with the sugar and bring to the boil, stirring continuously until the sugar dissolves. Thicken with the diluted cornflour. Stir in the cherries and gently warm through, add the rum or kirsch, if using.

To serve, drizzle each plate with some sauce Anglaise and melted chocolate. Turn the pudding out, place a dollop of whipped cream or ice cream on top. Make a slight dent in the middle of the cream or ice cream and spoon on the cherries. Decorate with a sprig of mint and dust with cinnamon sugar.

KW

IRELAND AND

The famous Golden Gate Bridge, gateway to San Francisco.

Organic is the name of the game here. Agricultural trends across Europe are for commercial-scale farms, with the aim of getting as high a yield from the land as possible. After the Second World War there was a great shortage of food, mechanization of farms was essential and with this came the need for higher crop yields and artificially fertilized soils. The organic way suits the laid-back attitude of the Irish and the fact that, in principle, quality is more important than quantity. This attitude, combined with naturally rich soil conditions, means that Ireland is one of the leading centres of organic farming in Europe.

In an American world of food chemical madness (a yoghurt I bought in the States had eight different chemicals on the label and yoghurt was third on the list of ingredients) California is striking out for a chemical free world and going organic, and not just organic but beyond organic. At his farm, Joseph Minocchi believes that vegetables should be grown in as stress-free conditions as possible. Not only does he grow organically in double beds (the plants have plenty of room), he's gone a step further and grows what the rest of the world would call weeds.

In an ideal world perhaps everything we eat would be grown without the assistance of artificial chemicals. I am sure with modern techniques that this would be possible, but once the chemical road has been taken it's difficult to go back.

RIGHT: *At Joseph Minocchi's farm in Healdsburg, near San Francisco.*

BELOW: *Cooking carageen moss on Ballyandreen Beach, Co. Cork.*

lemon and pepper oil

Flavoured oil is all the rage in California at the moment, and is so expensive. This delicate oil looks great and is very easy to make.

MAKES APPROX. 500 ML (1 PINT)

zest and juice of 2 lemons
475 ml (16 fl oz) olive oil
freshly cracked pepper

In a saucepan, reduce the lemon juice to 1 tbsp. Add the oil, heat to about 80°C/180°F, add the pepper and cover the pan. Immediately turn off the heat and leave the oil to cool. Once cold, whiz in a blender for 30 seconds, then pass the oil through a wire mesh conical sieve, pour into a bottle, add the lemon zest and cork the bottle. It will keep for several weeks.

KB

anchovy **vinaigrette**

This is a light dressing that will enhance any leaves you pull from the ground and call a salad. It doesn't need additional salt if you use cured anchovies, and surprisingly it doesn't taste too fishy, which I know some of my friends would be worried about.

MAKES APPROX. 250 ML (10 FL OZ)

175 ml (6 fl oz) olive oil
50 ml (2 fl oz) balsamic vinegar
3 garlic cloves, crushed
6 anchovy fillets, very finely chopped
freshly ground black pepper

In a bowl, whisk together all the ingredients. The vinaigrette may be tossed with your favourite combination of salad leaves.

KB

hearty **vegetable soup**

The great thing about this soup is that if you don't have the vegetables in the recipe, you can use what you do have.

SERVES 12

2.4 litres (4 pints) vegetable stock
1 pak choi, chopped
1 turnip, diced
1 cabbage, chopped
1 potato, peeled and diced
1 onion, diced
2 carrots, diced
1 red pepper, diced
1 yellow pepper, diced
1 tsp very finely chopped garlic
salt and freshly ground white pepper

In a large saucepan, place half of the vegetable stock and bring to the boil. Add one-third of the vegetables, cooking them for 10 minutes until they are tender. Remove the vegetables from the pan with a slotted spoon and place them in a food processor. Purée the vegetables with a small amount of stock until they liquefy.

Return the puréed mixture to the pan, and add the remaining vegetable stock. Bring to the boil and add the remaining vegetables with the garlic. Once the soup returns to the boil cover, reduce the heat and simmer for 30 minutes. Add salt and white pepper to taste.

KB

watercress and sorrel soup

I like to place a spoonful of sour cream in the centre of this soup when serving.

SERVES 4

6 tbsp olive oil
1 medium onion, diced
225 g (8 oz) red potatoes, peeled and diced
900 ml (1½ pints) vegetable or chicken stock
450 g (1 lb) watercress, without stems
225 (8 oz) sorrel, without stems
2 thick slices bread, cut into 2.5 cm (1 inch) cubes
salt and freshly ground black pepper

Heat 2 tbsp of the olive oil in a saucepan and add the onion and cook over a medium heat for 5 minutes until soft. Add the potatoes and stock and bring to a boil. Reduce the heat, cover and simmer for about 15 minutes until the potatoes are tender.

Stir in the watercress and sorrel, cover and simmer for 5 minutes, until the greens are wilted.

Purée the soup in a blender in batches and return to a clean saucepan. Reheat the soup over a medium heat and season with salt and pepper.

In a frying pan, heat the remaining 4 tbsp olive oil until hot. Add the bread cubes, and fry over a high heat until browned on all sides. Place on kitchen paper to drain. Serve the soup garnished with the croûtons.

KB

grilled **vegetables** with **balsamic** vinaigrette

This is a great dish to try out on the barbeque and, with a loaf of fresh bread, it could be a main meal. I always make more than I need because the vegetables are also good served cold with some feta cheese.

SERVES 8

4 plum tomatoes, halved
2 courgettes, cut into thick slices
1 aubergine, cut into round thick slices
1 red pepper, deseeded and cut into wedges
1 onion, cut into wedges
1 bunch kale
1 tbsp olive oil
4 tbsp balsamic vinegar
2 tbsp honey
1 tsp freshly ground black pepper
½ tsp salt
4 cloves garlic, very finely chopped

Place the tomatoes, courgettes, aubergine, pepper, onion and kale in an airtight container.

In a bowl, mix the olive oil, balsamic vinegar, honey, black pepper, salt and garlic. Pour the mixture over the vegetables and cover; marinate in the refrigerator for 1 hour, turning the vegetables twice during marinating.

Coat the grill rack with oil and grill the vegetables until the onion is tender, basting with the marinade.

KB

fennel and goat's cheese salad

These are two flavours from opposite ends of the taste spectrum that combine beautifully. I was really surprised at the quality of the goat's cheese I found in the UK. You are lucky, since American goat's cheese can be a little mild. When we visited Neal's Yard in London's Covent Garden, we tasted some really fruity goat's cheeses which would go well in this salad.

SERVES 4

1 large fennel bulb, thinly sliced
115 g (4 oz) goat's cheese, cut into 5 mm (¼ inch) slices
3 tbsp olive oil
salt and freshly ground black pepper

Soak the fennel slices in cold water for 10 minutes and drain, patting thoroughly dry. Spread the fennel on a platter and sprinkle with salt. Place the sliced goat's cheese on top, sprinkle with ground pepper, drizzle with the olive oil and serve.

KB

artichoke balls

Artichokes don't seem as popular in the UK as they are in the US; I guess people don't always know what to do with them. This recipe is so simple yet it is a great snack, or starter.

MAKES 48

350 g (12 oz) artichoke hearts
1 tbsp very finely chopped garlic
40 g (1½ oz) Italian breadcrumbs, plus extra for coating
40 g (1½ oz) Parmesan cheese, grated
6 tsp olive oil
salt and freshly ground black pepper

Finely chop the artichoke hearts in a food processor. In a bowl, mix the artichokes, garlic, breadcrumbs, Parmesan, olive oil and salt and pepper. Mix thoroughly. Form into balls and roll in the remaining breadcrumbs. Bake at 180°C/350°F/Gas 4 for 15 minutes.

KB

goat's cheese tartlet

In San Francisco we came across some really fresh organic goat's cheese. This tartlet uses that and my quick method for pastry. We served this with some tasty San Franciscan weeds, such as dandelion. If you want to go all the way, choose organic flour, butter and eggs.

MAKES 6

FOR THE PASTRY
225 g (8 oz) plain flour
½ tsp salt
115 g (4 oz) butter
120 ml (4 fl oz) ice water
1 egg white, beaten with 1 tsp of water

FOR THE FILLING
115 g (4 oz) crumbled goat's cheese
3 egg yolks
350 ml (12 fl oz) light cream
few drops of Worcestershire sauce
salt and freshly ground black pepper

Blend the flour, salt and butter until the mixture resembles fine breadcrumbs. Add just enough water to shape the dough into a ball. Also add the egg white with water to the dough.

Roll the pastry 3 mm/⅛ inch thick. Cut out pieces to fit into 7.5 cm/3 inch tartlet tins. Place the pastry in the buttered tins. Cover with circles of waxed paper and baking beans. Arrange the tins on a baking sheet and bake in a preheated oven at 230°C/450°F/Gas 8 for 10–12 minutes. Remove the paper and baking beans and bake for 3 minutes more. Turn off the heat. Keep the tarts in the oven with the door open for 1–2 minutes to dry thoroughly.

Fill the tart cases with the crumbled cheese. Whisk the egg yolks and light cream, season with the Worcestershire sauce, salt and pepper and pour over the cheese. Bake in a preheated oven at 230°C/450°F/Gas 8 for about 15 minutes, until firm.

KB

pasta with herb pesto

More so even than with other dishes, it is the quality of the ingredients that make the taste of this dish count. Make sure your pine nuts are really fresh – they go stale very quickly. Adjust the amount of pesto to your taste when tossing with the pasta.

SERVES 4

- 175 g (6 oz) fresh basil leaves
- 25 g (1 oz) fresh parsley
- 15 g (1½ oz) fresh oregano leaves
- 2 tbsp pine nuts
- 1 tbsp grated Parmesan cheese
- ¼ tsp salt
- 4 cloves garlic, peeled
- 2 tbsp olive oil
- 225 g (8 oz) pasta

In a food processor, place the basil, parsley, oregano, pine nuts, Parmesan, salt and garlic. Process until smooth and slowly pour in the olive oil, continuing to process until well blended.

Cook the pasta in a large pan of boiling salted water until al dente. Drain the pasta, and in a large bowl, toss the pasta with the pesto and serve.

KB

dandelion pasta

Would you ever have thought stems could taste so good?

SERVES 3–4

2 tbsp olive oil
50 g (2 oz) bacon, chopped
dandelion stems from 900 g (2 lb) of greens, cut into 2 cm/1 inch pieces
2 cloves garlic, sliced
225 g (8 oz) linguine
1 tbsp fresh lemon juice
pinch of crushed red pepper
salt
grated Parmesan cheese, to garnish

In a pan, heat the olive oil. Add the bacon and cook until crisp. Transfer the bacon to a plate. Add the dandelion stems to the pan and cook until crisp and tender, about 5 minutes. Add the garlic, cooking until lightly browned.

Cook the linguine in a large saucepan of boiling salted water until al dente. Drain the linguine and, in a warmed large bowl, toss the pasta with the dandelion stems, lemon juice and crushed red pepper. Season with salt and serve. Garnish with the bacon and Parmesan.

KB

dandelion and shiitake pizza

If you're a real pizza eater, then you'll love this – and just double the quantity to start with and make two.

SERVES 4–6

3 tbsp olive oil
115 g (4 oz) shiitake mushrooms, caps sliced 1 cm/½ inch thick
2 cloves garlic, sliced
450 g (1 lb) dandelion greens, stems removed
2 tbsp water
450 g (1 lb) ready-made pizza dough, divided in half
225 g (8 oz) fontina cheese
2 tbsp grated Parmesan cheese
salt and freshly ground black pepper

If you have a pizza stone or baking tiles, place on the bottom shelf of the oven and preheat to 240°C/475°F/Gas 9 for at least 30 minutes. If you do not have stone or tiles, bake the pizza on rimless baking sheets.

In a frying pan, heat 2 tbsp of the olive oil and add the shiitakes; cook for about 4 minutes until they brown. Add the garlic and stir until lightly browned. Transfer the shiitakes and garlic to a plate. Put 1 tbsp olive oil into the same pan, adding the dandelion greens and 1 tbsp water and cook for 3–4 minutes until wilted. Return the shiitakes and garlic with 1 tbsp water to the pan and cook until the liquid is absorbed and the greens are al dente. Season with salt and pepper then transfer to a plate.

On a lightly floured surface, stretch or roll the dough to form two 30cm/12-inch pizza rounds. Place the dough rounds on a floured rimless baking sheet. Brush the dough lightly with olive oil. Sprinkle one quarter of the fontina onto the dough. Top with half of the dandelion mixture and another quarter of the fontina. Sprinkle with 1 tbsp Parmesan. Repeat with the remaining ingredients on a second rimless baking sheet.

Shake the baking sheets to release the pizza and slide it onto the pizza stone. Bake in a preheated oven at 240°C/475°F/Gas 9 for about 10 minutes until the dough is crisp and topping is bubbling. Transfer to a rack, cut and serve.

KB

sweet potato and beef stir fry

Early San Franciscan Chinese settlers were essentially Cantonese. This dish is from the Cantonese *tsap sui* (Chop Suey), which means 'miscellaneous leftovers'. It is great made with chicken, pork or vegetables. Of course, it is a useful way to clean out the refrigerator, using all those ingredients that, alone, aren't enough for a meal.

SERVES 4

450 g (1 lb) boneless beef sirloin, cut into 5mm/¼ inch slices
175 ml (6 fl oz) chicken stock
50 ml (2 fl oz) hoisin sauce
2 tbsp brandy
1 tbsp cornstarch
4 tbsp peanut oil
1 red onion, thinly sliced
3 cloves garlic, sliced
2 large sweet potatoes, peeled, cut lengthways into 3 mm/⅛ inch slices, then cut into strips
350 g (12 oz) snow peas, cut in half
115 g (4 oz) whole water chestnuts, cut into 3 mm/⅛ inch slices
4 spring onions, sliced
2 tsp sesame oil
salt and freshly ground black pepper
flat leaf parsley and spring onions, to garnish
cooked rice, to serve

Season the beef with salt and pepper. In a small bowl, stir together stock, hoisin sauce, brandy and cornstarch until well mixed.

Heat a wok or heavy frying pan over a high heat until a bead of water dropped into the pan evaporates immediately. Add 2 tbsp of the peanut oil to coat the pan evenly and heat until hot but not smoking. Add the onion and stir-fry until softened. Add the garlic, then sweet potatoes stir-frying until just tender, 6–8 minutes. Add snow peas and water chestnuts stir-frying for 2 minutes. Transfer the vegetables to a large bowl.

Add 1 tbsp peanut oil to the pan and heat until just smoking. Stir-fry half the beef until browned and place in the bowl with the vegetables. Add remaining peanut oil and stir-fry the remaining beef; transfer to the bowl.

Add the stock mixture to the wok or frying pan and bring to a boil. Simmer for 1 minute, stirring, and return beef-vegetable mixture with spring onions to the pan and stir-fry until combined and heated through. Season with salt and pepper and stir in the sesame oil. Serve over rice, and garnish with flat leaf parsley and green onions.

KB

black and white pudding with celeriac potato mash and a grain mustard devilled sauce

This is comfort cuisine at its best, and one of my favourites after a hard day on the road.

SERVES 4–6

FOR THE CELERIAC POTATO MASH
1 celeriac, weighing about 450 g (1 lb)
675 g (1½ lb) potatoes
25 g (1 oz) butter
90 ml (3 fl oz) milk or cream
salt and freshly ground black pepper

FOR THE PUDDINGS
2 black puddings, weighing about 275 g (10 oz) each
2 white puddings, weighing about 275 g (10 oz) each
1 tbsp oil
25 g (1 oz) butter
2 tbsp chopped lovage or parsley, to garnish

FOR THE DEVILLED SAUCE
50 g (2 oz) butter
50 g (2 oz) onion, finely chopped
50 g (2 oz) carrot, finely chopped
50 g (2 oz) celery, finely chopped
1 bay leaf
1 sprig of thyme
1 tbsp tomato purée
100 ml (3½ fl oz) stout
2 tbsp red wine vinegar
300 ml (½ pint) brown stock
1 tsp wholegrain mustard
coarsely ground black pepper

Make the mash; peel and cut the celeriac into chunks, cover with lightly salted water and cook until tender. At the same time, in a separate pan, cook the potatoes. When cooked, drain well and dry out a little by placing the pan over a gentle heat. Mash the celeriac and potatoes together, add the butter and enough milk to reach a consistency that you like, and adjust the seasoning with salt and pepper.

Make the devilled sauce; melt 25 g (1 oz) of butter in a small saucepan, add the onion, carrot, celery, bay leaf and thyme, stir with a wooden spoon until slightly brown. Add the tomato purée, cook for 2 minutes and then add the stout. Allow the sauce to bubble until it has reduced by a good half. Add the vinegar and pepper and reduce further. Add the brown stock and simmer for 15–20 minutes. Strain the sauce and return to the saucepan, correct the seasoning with the pepper and wholegrain mustard. Finish the sauce with the remaining 25 g (1 oz) of butter.

For the black and white pudding; slice the black and white puddings at an angle into 2.5 cm (1 inch) pieces. Heat the oil and butter in a frying pan (or dry fry in a griddle pan), fry the slices until golden and thoroughly heated through.

To serve, make the mash into a cake in the centre of each plate and place the slices of pudding on top; garnish with a few sprigs of lovage or parsley leaves. Spoon the sauce around the outside of the plate and serve immediately.

KW

steak, kidney and guinness and mushroom pudding

There is something wonderfully British about a steak and kidney pudding. The fact that the ingredients cook in a sealed dish for over 4 hours is indicative of the flavours that will be unleashed once you break through the pastry. In addition, the Guinness gives a real depth to the sauce.

SERVES 4

FOR THE PASTRY
350 g (12 oz) self-raising flour
175 g (6 oz) shredded suet
1 tbsp tarragon, finely chopped
pinch of salt

FOR THE FILLING
2 tbsp plain flour
450 g (1 lb) chuck steak, diced
175 g (6 oz) kidney, diced
75 g (3 oz) mixed mushrooms, roughly chopped
115 g (4 oz) onions, finely diced
2 tbsp Worcestershire sauce
2 bottles Guinness or strong stout
salt and freshly ground black pepper
mashed potatoes and Brussels sprouts, to serve

Make the pastry; mix together the flour, shredded suet, tarragon and a little salt. Make a well in the centre and add sufficient cold water to make a smooth dough.

Roll out three-quarters of the pastry and use to line a 1.2 litre (2 pint) pudding basin or 4 dariole moulds, which have been greased.

Make the filling: dust the flour over the diced meat and kidney, shake off any surplus flour, add the mushrooms and onions; mix together and season. Put the mixture into the pastry-lined pudding dish and add the Worcestershire sauce, followed by just enough Guinness or stout to cover the meat.

Roll out the remaining pastry, dampen the edges with a little cold water and place on top of the pudding. Seal the edges by nipping the pastry together. Place a circle of greaseproof paper over the top and cover the whole pudding dish with a double layer of foil. Place in a steamer or double saucepan and cook for 5 hours.

To serve, unmould onto a large serving plate; serve with mashed potatoes and lightly cooked Brussels sprouts.

KW

studded **beef fillet** with a casserole of **mushrooms**

This is a substantial and very tasty dish, it makes a wonderful alternative to a traditional Sunday lunch.

SERVES 4

675 g (1½ lb) beef fillet, trimmed
7.5 g (3 inch) piece fresh ginger root, peeled and cut into thin strips
4 cloves garlic, cut into thin strips
olive oil
juice of ½ lemon
50 ml (2 fl oz) white wine vinegar
25 g (1 oz) shallots, finely chopped
1 tbsp chopped flat leaf parsley
3 egg yolks
175 g (6 oz) unsalted butter, clarified
450 g (1 lb) wild mushrooms, sliced
3 cloves garlic
4 spring onions, finely diced
1 tbsp chopped tarragon
1 glass Vermouth
1 stalk lemon grass, bruised
450 g (1 lb) potatoes, peeled
115 g (4 oz) onions, grated
vegetable oil, for deep and shallow frying
salt and freshly ground black pepper

Using a small sharp knife make a series of small incisions all over the fillet, penetrating deep into the flesh. Insert pieces of ginger and garlic into alternate incisions. Brush a little olive oil over the fillet and season with salt and freshly ground black pepper. Cover and leave at room temperature.

Place the lemon juice, wine vinegar, shallots and chopped parsley in a pan and heat until the liquid is reduced to about 1 tbsp.

Place the egg yolks into a mixing bowl, add the reduced vinegar mixture and whisk over a bowl of boiling water, taking great care not to overheat the eggs or they will curdle. Once the mixture has increased in volume by one-third, then begin slowly to add the butter whilst whisking. It may be necessary to move the bowl off the heat if it appears that the egg mixture is getting too hot. Once all the butter has been added, remove from the heat and then season the sauce very lightly with salt and freshly ground black pepper.

Heat a little olive oil in a shallow roasting dish over a high heat. Once very hot, add the beef fillet and seal, lightly colouring on all sides. Place in a preheated oven at 220°C/425°F/Gas 7 and cook for 15–20 minutes (depending how you like your beef cooked). Remove the beef fillet from the oven and allow to rest for 5 minutes.

Meanwhile heat 4 tbsp of olive oil in a frying pan, add the sliced mushrooms, garlic, spring onions and tarragon, and cook for 5 minutes. Add the Vermouth and bruised lemon grass and cook for a further 8–10 minutes. Remove and discard the lemon grass.

continued overleaf

Grate two-thirds of the potatoes, squeeze out the excess moisture and mix the potato with the grated onions. Season with salt and freshly ground black pepper. Using a mandolin or food processor, finely shred the remaining potatoes into very thin strips, deep fry these and reserve for garnish.

Divide the grated potato and onion mixture into 4 portions and place in a hot frying pan containing a little hot oil. Press down gently with a palette knife and cook for 4–5 minutes on each side.

Mix the egg and butter sauce with the mushroom mixture.

To assemble, place a potato and onion rösti on the centre of the plate. Carve a thin slice of beef and place on top of the rösti. Neatly disperse the casserole of mushrooms around the outer edge of the dish. Garnish by piling the deep fried potato on top of the beef and serve.

KW

orange sorbet

I often serve this as a refresher between courses.

SERVES 4

475 ml (16 fl oz) fresh orange juice
2 tsp grated orange zest
200 g (7 oz) sugar
1 tbsp lemon juice
1 tbsp vodka

In a metal bowl, combine the orange juice, zest, sugar, lemon juice and vodka. Place the bowl over a larger bowl filled with ice water. Stir to dissolve the sugar. It will take a few minutes and you can feel the bottom of the bowl with your finger to see if the sugar has dissolved.

Pour the chilled mixture into the container of an ice cream machine and churn until frozen. Place the frozen sorbet into a container with a good seal. Put the container into the freezer for several hours to allow sorbet to firm up.

KB

whiskey and oatmeal ice cream

This dish works equally well with Irish whiskey or Scotch whisky and oats – it always conjures up memories of summers in the Highlands of Scotland when my children were younger and, more recently, strolling through the heather with Big Kev.

SERVES 8

115 g (4 oz) medium oatmeal
750 ml (1¼ pints) milk
115 g (4 oz) caster sugar
4 egg yolks
Irish whiskey or Scotch whisky, to taste

Lightly toast the oatmeal under a grill, moving it around until it is just coloured and leave to cool.

Place the milk in a pan and bring to the boil. In a bowl, whisk together the sugar and egg yolks. Slowly pour on the hot milk, stirring continuously. Place the pan over a low heat and stir until the sauce coats the back of the spoon. Add the oatmeal and whiskey, mixing thoroughly.

Allow the mixture to cook. Use either an ice cream machine or place in an airtight plastic container in the freezer and stir every 30 minutes, until set.

KW

ragout of **spiced plums** in an irish **whiskey** sauce

You may need to add a little more sugar and honey if the plums are less sweet. I use plums which are just ripe as these release lots of flavour, whilst retaining their shape and a degree of sharpness (which I like). I also like to use this recipe as a filling for pancakes.

SERVES 4–6

50 g (2 oz) butter
675 g (1½ lb) plums, stoned
115 g (4 oz) soft brown sugar
pinch of mixed spices
pinch of cinnamon
finely grated zest and juice of 1 orange
4 tbsp Irish whiskey
1 tbsp honey

Heat the butter in a frying pan, add the plums and cook for 2–4 minutes. Add the sugar, spices and cinnamon and continue to cook until the sugar has dissolved, but before it turns to caramel.

Add the orange rind, pour in the whiskey and carefully set alight to burn off the alcohol, then add the orange juice. When the liquid begins to boil, reduce the heat and simmer for 2–3 minutes. Add the honey to taste (you may need a little less or more depending on your taste) and continue to cook until the liquid is syrupy.

This is lovely warm or cold especially when served with Carageen Moss Cream, or one of my speciality ice creams.

KW

pineapple **sorbet**

When I want a refreshing dessert, this is perfect!

SERVES 4

1 pineapple, peeled, cored and cut into chunks
150 g (5 oz) sugar
1 tbsp lemon juice
1 tbsp vodka or rum

Purée the pineapple in a food processor until smooth. Take out any stringy pieces.

In a metal bowl, add the pineapple purée, sugar, lemon juice, vodka or rum. Place the metal bowl over a larger bowl filled with ice water. Stir to dissolve the sugar. It will take a few minutes and you can feel the bottom of the bowl with your finger to see if the sugar has dissolved.

Pour the chilled mixture into the container of an ice cream machine and churn until frozen. Place the frozen sorbet in a container with a good seal. Put the container into the freezer for several hours to allow sorbet to firm up.

KB

carageen moss cream

Carageen moss is amazing and is used in Ireland for many healthy recipes and pick-me-ups. It is available in some health food shops and is a fascinating substance which is great to experiment with, so give it a try – it can only do you good. It's lovely served with my Ragout of Spiced Plums in an Irish Whiskey Sauce (see page 182).

SERVES 4–6

15 g (½ oz) dried carageen moss
500 ml (17 fl oz) milk
1 vanilla pod, split
zest of 1 orange, in strips
2 eggs, separated
50 g (2 oz) sugar

Wash the carageen in warm water and let it soak for 5–10 minutes. Place the carageen in a pan with the milk, vanilla pod and a few strips of orange zest. Bring to the boil and simmer gently for 15–20 minutes.

Pass the milk through a fine mesh strainer, extracting all the gelatine from the carageen. Whilst the liquid is still hot, whisk in the egg yolks and sugar. Cool slightly.

Stiffly whisk the egg whites and fold into the mixture. Spoon into one large or individual small moulds and chill for at least 4–6 hours.

KW

irish style pick-me-up with a cold **chocolate** sauce

This is my 'naughty but nice' recipe – it is an adaptation of the Italian classic, Tiramisu, but with a cunning twist. If you generally eat a low fat diet and therefore find a large amount of cream difficult to digest, this is for you. The carageen moss cream is much lighter than dairy cream and yet you still get the feeling of sheer indulgence from this sweet.

SERVES 4–6

2 sachets espresso coffee
24 sponge fingers or 275 g (10 oz) Madeira sponge, thinly sliced
90 ml (3 fl oz) Irish whiskey liqueur or coffee liqueur
1 amount Carageen Moss Cream (see page 185)
115 g (4 oz) dark chocolate, grated
4 tbsp whipped cream
fresh strawberries or raspberries, to decorate

FOR THE CHOCOLATE SAUCE
200 ml (7 fl oz) water
115g (4 oz) golden caster sugar
50 g (2 oz) cocoa powder
120 ml (4 fl oz) double cream

Using the coffee sachets, make a strong cup of coffee with 250 ml (8 fl oz) of boiling water, leave to cool a little.

Lay a third of the sponge or Madeira cake over the base of a bowl (or use individual balloon glasses for a stunning effect). Soak with coffee and some of the liqueur and then cover with a third of the carageen moss cream and grated chocolate. Repeat this process until you have three layers.

Cover and chill in the refrigerator for at least 2–4 hours.

To make the chocolate sauce, bring the water to the boil with the sugar and the cocoa powder. Take off the heat, add the cream, mix thoroughly and strain through a fine sieve. Leave to chill.

To serve, place a generous dollop of cream on the top, add a little of the chocolate sauce and decorate with some fresh strawberries or raspberries.

KW

blueberry coffee cake
with streusel topping

I really like blueberries, but if you want you can try different berries. There is no coffee in the cake itself, but it tastes great with a cup.

FOR THE TEABREAD
275 g (10 oz) flour
275 g (10 oz) sugar
1 tsp salt
275 g (10 oz) butter
2 tsp baking powder
175 ml (6 fl oz) milk
2 eggs
1 tsp vanilla essence
115 g (4 oz) blueberries

FOR THE FILLING
225 (8 oz) ricotta cheese
1 egg
2 tbsp sugar
1 tbsp grated lemon zest

FOR THE TOPPING
50 g (2 oz) chopped nuts
65 g (2½ oz) brown sugar
1 tsp cinnamon

Mix the flour, sugar and salt in a large bowl and cut in the butter. Reserve about 1 cupful of this mixture to use in the topping.

Add the baking powder, milk, eggs and vanilla to the remaining quantity and mix in a food processor or mixer on medium speed for 2–3 minutes. Pour into greased 23 x 33 cm/9 x 13 inch baking tin, then sprinkle the blueberries over the mixture.

Make the filling. Blend the ricotta cheese, egg, sugar and lemon zest until smooth and spread over the blueberries.

Mix the reserved flour and butter mixture, the nuts, brown sugar and cinnamon. Sprinkle over the ricotta layer. Bake at 180°C/350°F/Gas 4 for 50–60 minutes. Cool for 15 minutes before cutting.

KB

cranberry **pound cake**

In the States a pound cake is a plain, slightly sweet cake, usually made in a one-pound loaf tin. This is my version for a cup of tea and a slice. The cranberries mean it is not quite so sweet.

SERVES 10

FOR THE CAKE
115 g (4 oz) butter, softened
200 g (7 oz) sugar
2 eggs
225 g (8 oz) flour
1 tsp baking powder
1 tsp baking soda
½ tsp salt
250 ml (8 fl oz) sour cream
1 tsp almond essence
115–225 g (4–8 oz) cranberries
50 g (2 oz) chopped nuts

GLAZE
75 g (3 oz) icing sugar
½ tsp almond essence
1 tbsp hot water

Cream the butter and sugar until smooth and beat in the eggs well. Mix the flour, baking powder, baking soda and salt in a bowl. Gradually add the dry ingredients, alternating with the sour cream. Add the almond essence and cranberries.

Pour the mixture into a greased and floured 25 cm/10 inch tube pan. Sprinkle the chopped nuts on top and bake in a preheated oven at 180°C/350°F/Gas 4 for 1 hour. Cool for 10 minutes and turn the cake out onto a plate.

Mix the sugar, almond extract and hot water in a bowl and pour the glaze over the completely cooled cake.

KB

index

acknowledgements

Kevin Woodford would like to thank the cameraman Nick Manley and sound recordist Trevor Hotz for their technical genius and companionship while on the road.
Kevin Belton would like to thank his partners Bruce Trascher and Greg Leighton and the entire staff of the New Orleans School of Cooking and Riverview Room for being very supportive; and all his friends whom he did not telephone or write to for months because he was busy, for being so understanding.
The publishers would particularly like to thank Andrew Fettis for all his help in the creation of this book.